El Roi

The God Who Sees

Compiled by
Living Parables of Central Florida

El Roi

The God Who Sees

ISBN 978-1-963611-87-8

Cover Design: Robin Black

All interior images by https://clipart-library.com/free/god-clipart-black-and-white.html

Published by EA Books Publishing a division of
Living Parables of Central Florida, Inc. a 501c3
EABooksPublishing.com

ACKNOWLEDGMENTS

We'd like to thank Carol Kent and Bonnie Emmorey for the training and support through the Speak Up Conference. We thank Cheri Cowell and her wonderful team at EABooks Publishing for giving us this opportunity and our many friends and family for supporting us in our writing dreams. Most importantly, we want to thank our Lord and Savior, Jesus Christ, for His gifts—may this book bring you the honor and glory you deserve.

TABLE OF CONTENTS

NOTE FROM THE PUBLISHER

It is a daunting thing to submit your writing to a publisher. Doubts and fears prevent many from following their dream of becoming a published author. But these brave souls persevered. They overcame those doubts and fears, and they submitted. Then they waited. Those chosen for inclusion have followed their dream, submitted to the process, and are now published authors. We are proud of them and are grateful you've joined them in celebrating this milestone. As you read, my you find a reminder that God sees you, He is your — El Roi.

El Roi

The God Who Sees

Compiled by
Living Parables of Central Florida

Traces of His Hand

Juliana C. McFadden

*Really, God! Don't you see what has happened? Where were you?
Clearly nowhere to be found. Now, I am supposed to pray? No —
I'm done with you!*

That was my last conversation with God for nearly
seventeen years. The pain and horror of the murders,
coupled with my new reality, were too much to make sense
of. I felt hopeless. My escape was drugs, alcohol, and men.

I couldn't work; it was too much for me. I was
embarrassed and ashamed of my life and my family.
Especially my brother—for what he did. Who could I ever
tell? How would people see me? The fear of being revealed
as the sister of a murderer haunted me. Sorrow and remorse
for his victims overshadowed every part of my life.

I resigned from my secretarial job and became a
bartender, which gave me quick cash. When I didn't have
cash, there were men with cash, coke, and Jack. My life spun
out of control, and it got crazy fast.

Soon after my brother received his death sentence for the
triple murders, I was off to Dallas. I was done with Chicago.
I needed a geographical change. I think the night in jail at
11th and State was the kicker. It was a nonsense
misdemeanor, but real, nonetheless. Little did I know God
was qualifying me for a ministry in which He was shaping
me to serve.

In Dallas, I met David. Yep, another bad boy. I even
quickly nailed a bartender job at a topless bar. Daily life was

a party with David, and just about the time we began mainlining coke, I found out I was pregnant. I needed to go home.

David followed me to Chicago, and soon after, we were married. Then, three months later, our daughter Jennifer was born. Once again, my life was forever changed, but this time with a gift I could have never imagined.

David and I slowly built our life together with Jennifer. Like the seasons that effortlessly change in the Midwest, we successfully established our roots and flourished. We bought a home and had our second daughter, Kelly—another gift of new life!

We purchased property on a lake where we enjoyed endless weekends in our boat and camper, sitting around nightly bonfires while the children explored corn-lined country roads on their bikes. May transitioned to October, and as the winter snow relentlessly fell, we surrendered to being cocooned indoors until the season turned the key to reopening spring.

But by the fall of 1998, we had enough. Another geographical move was in order. Family in Phoenix, Arizona, inspired us to pack up and become Phoenicians. I was elated that there would be no more *snow* for us.

The drive to Phoenix was exhausting and exciting. Jennifer was preparing to start middle school, and Kelly was entering the third grade. David and I had provided our girls with a beautiful new home, and we could give them everything they could ever need or want.

That's when God spoke loud and clear to me; "That's great, but you have not given them the most important thing—they need Me!"

I could hear a pin drop in my head. I was silent for a bit, then replied, "Okay. You are right."

I yielded, and I made a promise to God. At this time, I was not attending church, but I promised God I would take the girls. A drop-off and pick-up, that's it.

The telephone rang as I got things together to pick the girls up from Wednesday night church. The police advised me that they had David in custody.

Bewildered, I asked, "Why?"

The officer proceeded, "Mr. McFadden was involved in a head-on car crash. He is okay, but the victim is hospitalized with injuries."

Victim?

"Wait!" I continued, "Why is David in custody if there was a car accident?"

The officer responded, "Ma'am, it appears Mr. McFadden may have been under the influence during the crash. You can come pick him up at the station."

My mind was racing with questions and emotions. This unexpected event would significantly shift my journey, leading me to a path I never anticipated.

As the story unfolded, I learned David had fallen asleep at the wheel while under the influence of opiates and hit the Mercedes head-on. In just a year and a half from moving to our new home in Phoenix, David was charged with aggravated assault and received a two-and-a-half-year prison sentence.

"Anne Graham Lotz is in town; do you want to go to the *Just Give Me Jesus* revival with me?" my friend Joanne asked.

"I have no idea who Anne Graham Lotz is," I replied.

"Oh! She is Billy Graham's daughter."

"I see. Okay, I guess so," I replied, hoping God would tell me if I should stay with my husband.

By now, David had been in prison for over a year, and during that time, I'd started attending church with our girls. It didn't make sense to drive them there, drop them off, drive home, drive back to get them, and then drive home again. It was just easier to stay for the service.

Joanne was a church lady who had befriended me. She was sweet and caring. So off we went. The funny thing is Anne Graham Lotz never said a word about whether I

3

should stay with my husband. But the Holy Spirit spoke clearly through her that night, November 10, 2001. Divorce was off the table.

My life was such a mess. My brother was in prison, and now, my husband was, too. I was exhausted, and self-medicating was not an option. I knew I needed Jesus because I once personally knew Jesus.

As I pondered Jesus and all He had done despite my wreckage, I knew I was done being angry with God. At this point, I needed Jesus more than anything in this world. Then I prayed, and in the blank spaces of the tear-off bookmark in the event program, I wrote, "I have decided to surrender my life to God—my will for His will. I commit myself to serve Christ."

This bookmark remains in my Bible today and serves as a "stone of remembrance" of my commitment that day (Joshua 4:21–24).

Shortly after David went to prison, I also began attending Al-Anon meetings for those who love someone struggling with addiction. One night, a year after I began attending them, the leaders announced that they needed volunteers to host Al-Anon Meetings at Perryville Prison for women in Goodyear, Arizona.

God would not relent about this new thing I could do to serve Him. "God, there is no way I'm going to visit anyone in prison, especially people I don't know!"

God said, "But you love people who are in prison." I said, "Actually, I do not."

I had not talked to my brother, Charlie, in years, and I barely wanted to speak to my incarcerated husband. I continued, "No, God. I am not doing that."

He said, "Try it, and if you don't like it, you can quit."

Reluctantly, I agreed, but I assured God that if it was too much for me—I was out! But as God would have it, I ended up serving women at Perryville Prison for the next six years.

In 2002, the *Purpose Driven Life* book by Rick Warren was the rage. I read it as part of our church initiative. Rick Warren wrote, "God wants you to have a Christlike ministry on earth. That means other people are going to find healing in your wounds. Your greatest life message and most effective ministry will come from [1]your deepest hurts."

ading this made it clear that I didn't need to hide or be ashamed. Instead, I needed to tell the story of what I went through because only by my telling would others find healing in my wounds.

As I continued to pursue God, He led me to the story of Hagar (Genesis 16:13). Hagar's cry to El Roi assured me that God had seen everything!

Seeking godly counsel, I shared my story with my pastor. In response, he uttered these simple words: "God has shaped your whole life for a time such as this" (Esther 4:14).

He pointed out the traces of God's hand in my life. Through His refining fire, God shaped me into something bigger for His kingdom (Malachi 3:2). Something that the enemy meant for harm, God meant for good (Genesis 50:20). On that day, I learned my purpose—that I was to be a missionary for Christ, used to pioneer a new model of ministry sharing the love of Jesus with formerly incarcerated women (2 Corinthians 5:17).

In 2006, SISTER Ministries, Inc. was born and subsequently incorporated as a 501c3 non-profit. Today, we celebrate eighteen years of service and, to date, have reached for Christ over 490 women.

El Roi! Yes, God sees me—still.

---

[1] *The Purpose Driven Life* by Rick Warren (Grand Rapids, Mich.: Zondervan, 2002), 275

Juliana C. McFadden is the founder and CEO of SISTER Ministries, Inc. She received her paralegal certification from Roosevelt University, Chicago, and is currently employed as vice president and document specialist at one of our nation's largest banks. Juliana was married to David for thirty-seven years, until he entered heaven in July 2021. For more information visit: www.sisterministries.org

A Warm Touch on the Coldest Day

Kris Darrah

The LORD is my shepherd; I shall not want
He makes me lie down in green pastures.
He leads me beside still waters.

Psalm 23:1–2, ESV

The words hung in the frigid January air as the small group of us stood huddled under the tent, shivering, making a feeble attempt to sing. Somehow, the song rang empty in my soul. Everything around me seemed dead and gray, from the withered, dry grass at our feet to the stark, bare tree branches waving against the overcast sky.

I was grateful for the cold — the graveside service must be short. I wasn't sure how long I could handle standing there looking at the white casket in front of me, knowing that it contained the body of my twenty-one-year-old daughter — knowing that it would soon be lowered into the ground. Thankfully, because of the hardness of the earth, that would take place later. It would have been more than I could bear.

Pastor Chad stepped forward to say a few words, but I could not concentrate on them. All I could think about was how bitterly cold the wind felt and how I couldn't wait to return to the car. The heaviness of the rest of the day loomed ahead of me. *How will I get through Lexi's memorial service and then the reception?*

As Pastor Chad began a closing prayer, I shivered uncontrollably and nestled against my husband, Mike. Sobs threatened to burst out of me, but I swallowed them. *Don't think, don't think, don't think.*

"Amen." The prayer ended the service. *Finally, one part of this torturous day finished.* Now, on to the next. I was overwhelmed with the pressure to honor and celebrate Lexi well and felt compelled to write her a letter to read at the service. I wanted everyone to know what an amazing and unique person she was and how much she meant to me. I *needed* them to know; I had to do it. But another part of me just wanted to cower in the car and avoid the whole thing. *God, help me. God, are you even here?*

As I hurried toward the car, wind whipping through my hair, I pushed my hands deeper into my pockets. Through my light cotton gloves, I felt a piece of paper. A receipt, a piece of trash? I pulled it out to see what it was.

What I saw stopped me in my tracks. It was Lexi's handwriting.

Confused, I unfolded and looked closer at the paper in my hands. It was a church bulletin dated months ago. And it was full of Lexi's notes and doodles from that day's sermon. Lexi had always had trouble sitting still in class or church and was much better at focusing if she could write while she listened. I knew she had probably handed me the bulletin after church, and I had stuffed it in my pocket. *How was it that I hadn't noticed it until that very day, at that very moment?*

As we drove from the cemetery across town to the church, I read through Lexi's notes, tears swimming in my eyes, feeling disbelief that such a treasure had turned up. It was as if God had reached down to remind me that Lexi was indeed with Him, safe and sound. Here were her notes about Him and His Word to prove it. *God, you* are *here! You see me! You care!*

As I sat through the service, I held onto that piece of paper like I was holding Lexi's hand and God's hand at the same time. I smiled as her Youth With a Mission leader shared stories of her compassion and bravery as she had served on the mission field in Nepal. My heart leaped inside me as her cousins read short messages about how they looked up to her. I held on as Pastor Chad delivered a stirring gospel message, including her particular verse: Psalm 64:5:

Blessed is the one you choose and draw near to dwell in your courts!
We shall be satisfied with the goodness of your house, the holiness of your temple!

It was a verse that had delivered Lexi out of a very dark time and had become one of her favorites. And now it spoke to us, as a reminder from His Word, that Lexi was dwelling in His courts, enjoying the goodness of His house and the holiness of His temple. Another sign of God's provision and His love is directly through the Bible. Oh how wonderful to feel His gentle and caring hand through His written Word. This time, God was speaking through His Word to our very hearts. What beautiful reassurance of His provision and His love.

With a deep breath and strength that could only come from God, I got up with my husband, Mike, by my side and shared my letter with Lexi. And I survived.

As I look back on that day six years ago, I remember the shattered and lonely person I was. I remember the deep, unrelenting pain that overwhelmed my entire soul. I remember the fear and dread of looking to the future, which felt like an impossible, formidable mountain that I would never be able to climb.

But what a joy to remember the treasure of those notes in my pockets. What a pleasure to remember the verse that reassured us of Lexi's heavenly home. During so many challenging moments, those became a reminder of God's provision—that even though we may suffer through some awful times, God is right there beside us. He has not forgotten us. He will be faithful to reveal Himself when we cling to Him. When we know our Creator is there, we can survive anything.

In the days, months, even years to follow, as I struggled through some tough times, the reminder of Lexi's sermon notes found that day often pulled me through. It was a reminder that God is always there, even if we don't always feel Him. A reminder that He will always provide the sustenance we need to get through if we just keep holding on and relying on Him. God is faithful.

Kris Darrah is an English teacher, wife, and mother of four adult children (three are still being sanctified and one is already glorified). She has a passion for proclaiming God's healing power to those dealing with mental illness, substance use, suffering, and loss. Read her weekly blog at treasuresintrials.com.

This is Why

Tris Wojo

A couple of summers ago, I was in a car accident that left me with permanent, life-altering injuries. I was rear-ended and had just thought I was sore the following day.

Within the next couple of months, I became seriously ill. Slowly, over time, my major organs began having problems, and I was bedridden for three months. I had continuous testing and worried that my life was going to be like this forever. I fell to my knees in prayer, asking God for an answer. "Why is this happening?"

I had quit school, ended a relationship, and lost all my friends. My mom learned about a girl with the same symptoms affecting her major nerves, organs, and bones. The girl traveled a great distance for treatment, but I was fortunate enough to have a similar specialist in my city.

I began weekly treatment. Soon, I could manage my symptoms sufficiently and once again live as normal a life as possible.

Fast forward to this year, when I volunteered as a leader in my church's youth group. I instantly became very close to several students and learned that one had Ankylosing Spondylitis, a genetic disease involving the spinal bones fusing and severe arthritis. We discussed his newly found symptoms and how his life was changing.

"Why is this happening?" He asked.

I replied with my car accident story, explaining "This is why—God sees things that you don't understand quite yet. You repeatedly ask, 'Why?' and it feels like God isn't giving you an answer. Sometimes, no answer is the answer. Whenever God does not give an answer, He asks you to trust him. We live every day on fast replies and instant gratification, so it is difficult to have patience. He is telling you He sees and loves you, which is why He is brewing the perfect plan for your life."

I feel that this is true not only for him and me but also for you.

Jesus replied, "You don't understand now what I am doing, but someday you will" (John 13:7, NLT).

Tris Wojo is a 20-year-old student from Columbus, Ohio. She lives with her family and is studying secondary English education. In her free time, she enjoys different art mediums, such as drawing and film photography, volunteering as a youth leader, being on a worship team, and spending time with family.

When Sight Leads to Joy

Jennifer Sakata

Have you ever been blindsided—numerous times in one day, wondering if God sees you? That was my day yesterday.

One minute, I hugged and kissed our kids off to school. The next, my eyes flooded with tears amid the overwhelming plethora of everything. In a text I read, a miracle unfolded for a health issue in a friend's life while the cure remained distant for another.

Later, I sat with a friend in the coffee shop and replayed the pain of a distressing letter I sent to someone I love. In between sips, we celebrated the birth of my podcast, *Living the Grace Life,* while acknowledging the angst of distanced friendships and crumbling futures that resemble anything but grace.

During a phone call later in the day, I lamented the back and forth of God's goodness in contrast with His seeming absence. Our conversation left me spinning and looking for a safe place to land.

My soul was tired. I collapsed into an afternoon nap.

Did anyone see me?

Hagar understood well the seeming invisibility that comes with praise and pain. Genesis 16 tells us her story. She was an Egyptian slave girl forced into the toxic confusion of waiting and doubt. Unable to conceive God's promised heir to Abram, Sarai positioned Hagar to produce the son she could not. The view from Sarai's tent? Hagar was a means to an end. Nothing more. Nothing less.

In due time, Hagar became pregnant. Like the blooms of summer, she was adorned with the colors of motherhood — radiant with life as she carried this hoped-for child. But like expiring foliage, jealousy, and comparison reared their ugly heads, and life as Hagar knew it dried up. One moment, elevated; the next, exiled.

How often do we get tangled in the crossfires of someone else's longings and misguided efforts, tossed about by ulterior motives and mixed agendas? When it's not someone else's desires tossing us about, we get tripped by our own, landing us in arrogance or busyness that blurs our vision, leaving us isolated and hurting.

As we often do, Hagar sat alone in the wilderness, her insides suffering the clash of praise and pain. She sat down and wept—no doubt rehearsing all the ways she'd been ignored, used, and forgotten.

Moments later, an angel met her and asked a question God's heavenly messenger already knew the answer to: "Hagar, Sarai's servant, where have you come from and where are you going?" (Genesis 16:8, NLT).

It's a question of vision and purpose. Stated another way: "Hagar, what do you see going on here? What's this all about?"

I appreciate her honesty: "I'm running away from my mistress, Sarai" (Genesis 16:8, NLT). I imagine Hagar's internal dialogue went something like this: *I felt the joy of being wanted and seen and heard for a moment. But just like that, now mixed with arrogance I regret, I was tossed away as if I'd never been there. It's too much — too many demands. Nobody understands what it's like to have his or her choices stripped away — not like this. And who cares about the feelings of a foreigner whose job is to serve those around her, no matter the cost?*

God's messenger spoke into her pain and the disorienting heartache: "Return to your mistress, and submit to her authority. I will give you more descendants than you can count." And the angel also said, "You are now pregnant and will give birth to a son. You are to name him Ishmael (which means 'God hears.'), for the LORD has heard your cry of distress. This son of yours will be a wild man, as untamed as a wild donkey! He will raise his fist against everyone, and everyone will be against him. Yes, he will live in open hostility against all his relatives" (Genesis 16:11–12, NLT).

Despite the glib prospects the angel spoke of her son, Hagar rose as a woman who was seen, known, and heard. Her joy wasn't tied to Ishmael's future. Her joy unfolded in the presence of the One who saw her. Not as a slave. Not as a wife substitute. Not even as a woman about to bear a child.

Joy became her companion as she praised the One who saw her—for who she was. Praise bubbled up from the depths of her pain as Hagar became the first human to name God by the title *El Roi.*

"You are the God who sees me. Have I truly seen the One who sees me?" (Genesis 16:13, NLT). Yes, Hagar. God saw you. And yes, Hagar, you saw God.

Does Hagar's story remind you of others? There were the widow and the Shunammite woman of 2 Kings 4, whose lives were forever changed by God's miraculous compassion through Elisha. The voice of Hannah cried out to be seen and heard in a sea of women whose wombs were more generous than hers. Enter baby Samuel. There was the woman of Mark 12:41–44 and her two small coins. She captured the attention of Jesus when everyone else was blind to her minuscule offering.

Let us not forget the women at the Tomb after Jesus rose from the dead. Jesus first appeared to the women whose voices had been marginalized, not the wealthy or educated, nor the privileged nor the well spoken. Many years after Hagar's tears dried up, El Roi saw the hearts of those hurting from the outside edges of life.

God sees you, too, dear reader. Then and now. In the back and forth of praise and pain. For those moments that leave you feeling unseen, undone, or unprepared for what's ahead. When the joy of newborn nuzzles leads to the sorrow of a conflicted future. Or when the diagnosis cuts deeper than surgery. When hurt lays hidden beneath a lifetime of masking and moving on. And when the overwhelm of doing more and living less leaves you graceless, regretful of words you cannot take back.

In those moments, receive the kindly positioned eyes of God. El Roi, the God who cradles in compassion and gives voice to your silence. The God who understands and welcomes in. The God who won't ever stop loving you and never loses sight of you — not once.

A prayer for when praise and pain come crashing in:

El Roi,
You are the God who sees. You saw Hagar, and You see me — more clearly than I see myself. You see the sincerity of a celebrated heart. And You perceive my pain from people who tie me in knots or situations that leave me hopeless and despairing. In Your kindness, God, walk with me in both. Deepen my trust on those days when I'm tossed by the clash of praise and pain. Restore to me the joy of my salvation — the joy of being seen and heard and known and welcomed by You.

I belong to You, O Lord, now and forever. In Jesus' Name, Amen.

Jennifer Sakata is a joy-seeker who nurtures relationships at the intersection of real grace and real life. A speaker, author, and host of the *Living the Grace Life* podcast, Jennifer's passion is to replace the overwhelming cycle of "doing more" and living less with a slower pace that welcomes God's grace. Jennifer and her husband, Craig, raise their two earthside teen sons in Central Illinois. Connect with her at www.jennifersakata.com or on Instagram @JenniferSakata and Facebook @JenniferSakata.Author.

The Dam Breaks

Bonnie W. Chung

The eyes of the Lord watch over those who do right; his ears are open to their cries for help.

Psalm 34:15, NLT

I was seven months pregnant with my second child when my friend Joyce called, asking me to attend church with her that evening to view the Billy Graham movie *The Eye of the Storm*. She said they had childcare for my year-old son, and she could pick me up at 6:30 p.m. I gladly accepted and silently hoped this movie would answer my prayers.

Joyce was late picking up my son and me for the movie. The church was packed that evening, with barely any parking left. As I took my son to the childcare center, Joyce went to find our seats.

I entered the sanctuary and found her in the middle of the sanctuary, where she had saved me a seat in the dead center of the row. "Seriously, Joyce?" I mumbled.

I took a deep breath as I inched my way down the row, trying not to hit anyone with my heavily swollen pregnancy belly and thinking, *Why did I come?* I was tired, and my heart was aching as badly as my body; it was difficult to know which hurt worse. I found my seat just as the movie started.

Sixty-five minutes later, the movie ended, as did my hope. Nothing in the film spoke to my situation. I was defeated and tired, wanting nothing better than to go home, put my son to bed, and cry myself to sleep. The sooner, the better. As I stood, hoping Joyce would get the clue, the pastor took the podium.

I huffed and rolled my eyes as I sat back down. I listened impatiently, planning the best route for my escape as the pastor spoke about the movie. Before dismissing the congregation, he gave an altar call. He first called those who wanted to give their lives to Jesus. Then, he invited anyone going through the eye of a storm in his or her own life to come forward for prayer.

The music played as people began to go forward for prayer. My heart quickened as the Holy Spirit whispered for me to go forward.

No way! I replied.

"Come," He whispered a bit emphatically.

Nope. What will I pray for? I thought my needs were too many, and my heart was too broken.

Shaking my head and mumbling "No" to myself, I said to God, *No one knows; I would break down if I went for prayer; God, now is not the time! Besides, how would I ever get out of this row?*

Joyce gave me a quizzical look and said, "Why don't you go forward?"

I could only shake my head as I desperately tried to swallow my tears. I did not want anyone to know about my failures, hurt, or pain. One word from my mouth would break the dam I had built that held back my river of tears.

My spirit was tormented as the music continued playing. My resistance weakened as the Holy Spirit pressed further on my heart, drawing me forward. I finally said, *"Fine, God, I will go on one condition! I will go to the far corner of the altar where nobody is and pray by myself!"*

With my tongue sticking out at God in my mind, I inched my body and growing belly down the row and up the church aisle to the altar.

True to my word, I went to the very corner of the altar stairs where no designated prayer person was located. I slowly lowered my pregnant body to a step, placed my face into my hands, and then began praying.

Soon, I was surrounded by others who requested that someone pray with them, but I kept to myself and prayed. I did not need someone to pray for me. Many had prayed for me over the previous two years. I prayed every morning at 5 a.m. and fasted every Friday about my marriage, and still, my situation had gone from bad to worse.

I knew God was real, but I wasn't sure He cared. My bad marriage was on me, not God. At the marriage altar, my heart had said, "Run." As typical, I had stuffed that voice and feeling deep within my soul. I had known I should run, but my feet had stayed put.

I had messed up, and now I must live with the consequences of too many wrong decisions. I believed the saying, "You made your bed; now you must lie in it." (Whatever that means.) I was willing to lie in it, but I needed God to heal my broken heart.

I begged Him to help me. I did not know what to do and wondered if God even saw me or my pain. The only answer I'd received was silence. So, I'd responded by stuffing my pain and building a thick wall around my heart in hopes of suppressing all my pain.

I had obeyed the Spirit by coming forward to pray, and now it was time to wrap it up and leave. Just as I was doing that, I heard something. One of the prayer partners was praying for a man to my left. I did not know the woman praying nor had I seen her before. But every word out her mouth was as if it came from the mouth of God. Everything she prayed for this man was precisely a prayer I needed.

I began to listen more intently, silently agreeing with her prayer. Then the most unbelievable thing happened. She stopped mid-sentence, placed her hand on the man's shoulder, and said, "I am so sorry; this prayer is not for you."

I don't know who looked more dumbfounded—me or the man she prayed for. This woman placed her hand on me, looked deep within my soul, and said, "This prayer is for you."

Tears threatened to spill as my mouth fell open in disbelief. This kind prayer warrior asked me my name and continued her prayer, not for the man, but for me. She prayed for things that I had never told anyone about. She began talking to God about me, my hurting heart, and my deep hidden feelings and thoughts. It was like she was an angel from heaven sent to me by my Heavenly Father.

As she prayed, the dam broke, and I could not stop my tears or speak. But I did not need to talk; this woman told my heart to God. That night, she prayed God's words over me and to me. She encouraged me and said that God had heard all my prayers, that He saw me. She said He has been collecting all my tears. He had not forgotten me and had a plan for my life. She said that I had been believing a lie and needed to believe the truth.

I do not know how long she prayed for me, but when she finished, although I was spent, I had never felt more loved or seen than at that moment in time.

I slowly rose to my feet, gripping the crumbled ball of tissues in my hand and wiping away my tears. I then turned around to see that the place had emptied. I walked outside and found Joyce with my son, waiting patiently for me.

I still had tears as Joyce asked expectantly, "What happened?"

I smiled. Then, in an awe-inspired cracked voice, I whispered, "God sees me!"

She smiled a knowing smile that only a mature Christian smiles—someone who has been through an eye of a storm or two and knows that God's eye is always on His children.

Bonnie W Chung is a national speaker and author who resides in New England. She brings hope to those who have been knocked down by life, and helps them renew their hearts through the healing balm of Christ. You can reach Bonnie at www.bonnieWchung.com on Facebook or Instagram @bonniewchung or email at bonniewelchchung@gmail.com

By Lamplight

Kelly Wilbanks

God's first words on record,
"Let there be light," and
with these first words
He also created sight.

Did He want a lamp
to see His handiwork
creating oceans, fauna,
jungles, and deserts.

Then, man in His image
Love and Lover
incarnate, whole
Eyes for each other

And for assessing,
surveying, deciding,
weighing, conveying,
and vital aligning.

Every thought, expression
worn like a canvas
of the soul, Spirit
alive, bold innocence,

Before they grew hard
with knowledge and fear.
Eyes, a perfect reflection,
A revelation, a perfect mirror

So, many ways of seeing
in this world of lambs and lions
Of deep-sea dwellers and flyers,
prey and predators, and shepherds.

How did they see the world?
From light to frightening darkness,
From heights to ocean depths,
Varied vantages transgress.

How would my viewpoint change
If I had the poor vision of a kiwi
or the glowing eyes of a squid?
To know all this and yet see me.
How does seeing all illuminate,

inform and inspire an Intelligence.

A spinning spider, a salmon upstream

A butterfly wing, elephants.

Yet, He sees the motivations of my heart.

The upsets of governments and kingdoms.

He sees *me* as this tapestry,

Each step, as valued as His own

When hopelessness leaves me blind

And silences my joy, and I forget

to look for anchor points displayed:

A Douglas Fir, a frog, loves formed objects.

God created a world reflecting, revealing

His heart, His hope, and the healing

He built into His earth — all — this

— light, to share all — this — beauty.

The following verses contributed to the main ideas of this poem. These words remind me that God loves me specifically, not just universally, while His perspective is as varied as His creation's diversity. These reminders anchor me to other promises of God's goodness, gentleness, kindness, temperance, and peace. Being seen and, therefore, being known is the craving of every human heart — only in

God's Word do I see His message of love borne out so clearly.

Hebrews 4:13: "Nothing in all creation is hidden from God's sight. Everything is uncovered and laid bare before the eyes of him to whom we must give account."

Job 28:24: "For he views the ends of the earth and sees everything under the heavens."

Job 34:21 "His eyes are on the ways of mortals; he sees their every step."

Proverbs 5:21: "For your ways are in full view of the Lord, and he examines all your paths."

Psalm 139:13–16: "For you created my inmost being; you knit me together in my mother's womb. I praise you because I am fearfully and wonderfully made; your works are wonderful, I know that full well. My frame was not hidden from you when I was made in the secret place when I was woven together in the depths of the earth. Your eyes saw my unformed body; all the days ordained for me were written in your book before one of them came to be."

Kelly Wilbanks is a creative nonfiction writer living in Yakima, Washington, with her husband and three precocious daughters. She's written freelance articles for international publications and her town newspaper. Kelly is attending Central Washington University to complete her master's in professional and creative writing.

Lean In and Exhale

Lori Tuckerman

Hunched over in his chair with head in his hands, he looked at me with heavy tears streaming down his worn face. In raw transparency, he whispered, "Is God even with us anymore?"

Under bright fluorescent lighting, I sat with him in that sterile doctor's office as he began recalling everything he'd prayed for and how most prayers had not turned out as he'd hoped. As he proclaimed how exhausted his faith had become, I almost heard what was coming next before he even took his next breath, "Does God love me at all?"

Typically, when approached by hurting people who are questioning their faith, my strengths of positivity and empathy take over. I quickly pray to myself a "God, please let me say the *right thing*" prayer and move forward. I'm either quick to pull some guidance from how I feel led or, if nothing comes, offer friendship, support, and prayer to help point them toward possible answers.

This time was different. This time, I was looking into the swollen, tear-filled eyes of my husband. We had just received life-altering news from his doctor that ended with the words, "You have cancer."

The weight of the news was hard and heavy. We had only gone to the urologist for answers to our "whys" after five years of failed fertility treatments. A cancer diagnosis was a blow neither of us anticipated.

Our future was dramatically changed. Our dreams of having a child together were ripped out of our hands. Now, he was being prepped for a new battle — one that would turn him into a human pincushion full of toxic medicine in the hopes of keeping him alive.

It was all happening more quickly than we could have imagined. My head was spinning from the rapid pace of everything the medical teams planned and communicated. As they came in and out of the room to share unfavorable test results, it took all my strength to remind myself to breathe.

With every breath I took, I also had to remind myself to exhale, letting the air out again as I braced myself for the next bit of news from the doctors.

During the conversations with my husband after that devastating appointment, I continued to hear his outpouring of lost hope. Each time he spoke from the brokenness in his soul, I could only momentarily hold my breath and process what I was hearing.

However, I felt God's presence, even in my soul's sadness, chaos, and weariness. I wanted so badly for my husband to feel peace and comfort in this storm, so I'd circle my mind to retrieve verses containing evidence of hope. But his heart didn't budge — he said he felt *nothing.*

As treatment began, the light in his eyes grew dim. It was almost as if the chemotherapy was not only killing the cancer but also attacking his soul. The questions in his heart continued to pull him away. He was pulling away from God, his family, his friends, and everything I know my husband loves on this earth.

I was the exception. He pulled me in closer as he pulled away from God and everyone else. I knew I needed to take another deep breath and carry enough faith and hope for us both in those moments.

Let us hold tightly without wavering to the hope we affirm, for
God can be trusted to keep his promise. Let us think of ways to motivate one another to acts of love and good works (Hebrews 10:23–24, NLT).

As I was stretched and aching from carrying the weight of this battle, I watched the treatment tear through his body. It also continued wrecking his soul, breaking his heart, and leaving a void where his trust in God once lived.

I was laid low in the dust, and my own questions began to come: *How can I continue to do this? How do I keep my head up and remain strong and ready to fight for someone else's hope when mine is so beaten and tired?*

In despair, I cried out, and in response, I heard a whisper telling me to *lean in*.

Lean into Jesus. For answers.

For rest. For peace.

For words to share with my husband. Let go of the breath you've been holding. Exhale.

Prayerfully, I asked a question I already knew the answer to: "God, is it really *that* simple?"

YES!

Lean into Jesus. For *everything*. Lean into Jesus.

"Trust in the LORD with all your heart; do not depend on your

own understanding. Seek his will in all you do, and he will show you which path to take" (Proverbs 3:5–6, NLT).

It was as if this simple instruction had reached directly into my heart and lifted it above the darkness, trying to take over. I took my next breath, exhaling slowly, and I leaned in. This moment with God was pivotal in the days that followed.

I leaned in, and Jesus showed up. He answered my needs and provided strength when I was too weary to cry. The strength I found by leaning into all I knew to be true kept pushing me forward.

He also showed up in the people who showed up. I paused parts of my life to allow space and time for this fight. I called in my army of prayer warriors, family, friends, and neighbors. I learned to lean in and accept the help, love, prayer, and services those around us offered.

Friends surrounded me. They held me up by showing up at our doorstep with meals, mowing our grass, and sending encouraging text messages, cards, and emails filled with prayers, guidance, and love. It was like watching God's physical work on this planet done by the hands of those who follow Him.

I often read the messages aloud to my husband and felt the heavy weight and burden shift slightly. I held tightly to the hope that God would release my husband's worry, fear, and crushed spirit. I prayed daily he could find strength and faith in the Lord to fight.

"Surely you need guidance to wage war, and victory is won through many advisers" (Proverbs 24:6, NIV).

From the moment we heard the diagnosis, the battle had begun. Our lives shifted without our control. We continued to charge ahead on this path and eventually made it through the battle to defeat the enemy.

I look back to those first moments in that little room. I've always known that God *never* leaves us. He always loves us. He sees us in our strongest *and* our weakest moments.

He should not have had to tell me to lean in . . . I knew that already. My Bible study training of the past had taught me those truths. But in those moments, He saw what I needed and met me right where I was with the reminders of the truths I knew.

Leaning into Jesus gave me the strength to uphold my husband. The outpouring of love and support from family, friends, and neighbors allowed me to exhale when I needed to be lifted, too.

I'm continually grateful for those who stood next to us as we approached the front lines. Leaning in and trusting Jesus with His plan for our lives, even amid disappointments and heartbreaks, revealed strengths of my soul I didn't know existed.

Amid your struggles, remember those two simple words: *Lean in.* Jesus is always ready to catch you, hold you up, and care for you—even if you need Him to remind you on your most challenging days.

"*Finally, be strong in the Lord and in the strength of His might*" (Ephesians 6:10, ESV).

Lori Tuckerman is an author, business consultant, wife, mother, and dog mom. Writing is her passion. When she's not busy crafting tales of faith and love, you can find her taking long walks, reading, cooking, serving at church, and enjoying time with family and friends. Follow her on Instagram @loriloupensandproduce.

Breath of Life

Kelly Albrecht

I sat in a wheelchair in the hospital, thirty-eight weeks pregnant, moments away from experiencing my baby's first breath while tragically witnessing my dad's last breath.

Throughout my pregnancy, I battled a pregnancy illness that depleted my body, mind, and soul day after day. Each day was a struggle to care for myself and my other children. My husband would find me on the floor trying to feed our children but too weak to get up. I needed IVs weekly to function with little capacity.

I wrestled with why God didn't answer my prayers for a miracle when I prayed so much for it and for the desire to be grateful for this pregnancy. Sickness came to steal the experience of the miracle of pregnancy.

My dad was a wonderful gift to me during this pregnancy, holding my hand through all of it. He came to play with my young boys, who adored him, folded my laundry, and listened to me as I shared about another hard day. He rejoiced with me when I had a rare "good day" with less shortness of breath, fewer heart palpitations, and only one IV stick rather than eight attempts.

My dad's body was declining, but no doctor gave us the heads up to prepare ourselves for goodbye. Dad and I related to each other with the challenges of our spouses being our caretakers and the difficulty of getting out of breath just walking in our homes.

It was a strange feeling to approach the end of my journey with this sickness at the same time as my Dad's end of life, but his did not end with a new life on this earth. It ended with a new life in heaven.

In an already hard season of my life, I needed to say "See you later" to my beloved dad. In the days before Dad went to heaven, he shared how he'd planned that when he got out of the hospital, we could all go to the mountains — his favorite place. That day did not come. He went to the highest mountain to worship his Lord and Savior, but we didn't get to go with him. Instead, I felt left in the valley, my heart aching and confused.

Not even forty-eight hours after he breathed his last breath on earth, it was time for my baby to breathe his first breath on earth. Ready or not. . . . When those at my work suggested I take bereavement leave and have time to grieve, instead, I was pushing a baby out of my body.

While in labor, I remembered the weariness of the past nine months, especially the last couple of weeks of my dad in the hospital, and it hit me so hard as I was pushing. The "I can't do this" feeling and thoughts that are common in the transition stage of giving birth swirled in my mind. I said aloud, "I need Jesus to help me," instead of "I can't do this." My midwife kindly responded, "He is here."

And He was. The worship music playing and the pictures of mountains on the walls reminded me of that. He is the God who sees us and is with us, even in the most challenging seasons, especially when it feels like we just can't take anymore. He gives strength when we feel like we have no strength. His grace is indeed sufficient for us.

God gave me a beautiful baby boy in the Mountain Suite at the birth center. It was the suite I felt God encourage me to choose months before, not knowing my dad, who loved the mountains, would not meet this baby. God knew I would need reminders that He saw me and was with me, there to give me strength to birth my baby and there to comfort me as I mourned and deeply missed my dad.

God even gave me a baby who held my hand while nursing, comforting me as I missed holding my dad's hands. None of my other babies did that. God saw my need for comfort, and He met it most sweetly.

Although it felt at times that God didn't see me and that I was alone, in the most precious way, He reminded me that He saw me, was with me, and never left us.

Kelly Albrecht is wife to Josh, a chaplain in the US Airforce, and a momma to three boys: Joshie, Isaac, and Noah. Kelly is a licensed mental health counselor with a heart to help people remember that God sees them and is with them, even in the hardest seasons.

Mirror, Mirror on the Wall

Lisa Michelle Jones

Mirror, mirror on the wall, your reflection leads us to fall.
Mirror, mirror of the Word, your reflection makes His name heard

When did the mirror on the wall become more important than the mirror of God's Word?

The women walked in and out of the brightly lit bathroom. It looked more like a fashion show than a church.

I observed the women symbolically ask the mirror for what it couldn't give: affirmation of who they were. Mirror, mirror on the wall, who is the most beautiful of all?

I wondered about their thoughts and self-talk that followed as they left. I took my turn in front of the mighty reflector. I drew a deep breath, considering my relationship with the mirror, which had been complicated all my life.

I slowly exhaled, thanking God for how far I had come. For a few moments, I gratefully recalled the journey of replacing anxious thoughts with His Word daily, gradually allowing my escape from constant comparison, conscientious connections, and community camouflage.

My thoughts drifted back to a night in Arizona many years before. I had crawled out of bed, in the cover of darkness, and assumed my regular position on the floor in the dark. *Are 100 crunches enough? Or should go for 500?*

Who was I kidding? Nothing I did was ever enough. I already had enough mental "shoulds" for someone three times my age, and my goal was unrealistic. However, I knew

I must move quickly. Beverley, the medical health technician on duty, would be making rounds soon.

We were friendly with each other, but that wouldn't stop her from enforcing the rules. Shortly, she would sweep the beams from her flashlight across our room to ensure no one was doing exactly what I was doing. I felt confident enough to spring into bed when I heard her. Yet another unrealistic perspective.

Only in hindsight do I see how many unrealistic perspectives I harbored. If only I had recognized these distorted thought patterns and stopped their compounding effects. Instead, an eating disorder that tried to claim my life had landed me in a shared bedroom of a treatment center in Arizona, attempting 500 crunches without getting caught.

Years of denial built a wall thicker and higher than my conscious thoughts could climb or penetrate. Yet, glimmers of hope shone through gaps in that wall blown out by the One mightier than any fortress of my making.

El Roi, the God who sees, saw right through my wall, weaknesses, and wardrobe of identities. Through His faithfulness and sovereignty, the Arizona treatment center aligned me with His Word, will, and ways.

Thankfully, the God who sees me rescued me and taught me how to see. Eventually, I understood that releasing control and redirecting my trust to God instead of the wall around me made all the difference. It's never about *what* we are seeing. It's always about *how* we see it.

Be Aware of the Enemy's Filters

The enemy doesn't create; he twists. He bends our perception by layering filters over truth. Two of his most often used strategies are the filters of fear and shame. They are as thick as thieves and offer no shortage of filtered images and compromising situations.

When comparison and control drove me to the depths of a deadly disorder, I found myself hiding in shame, forcing

500 crunches of pain. Yet, when I learned to walk in the freedom of Christ, allowing Him to show me how He sees me, I began to see life unfiltered.

Filtering the truth is a familiar strategy. The enemy used it for the first time to cause humanity's fall. After Adam and Eve ate the forbidden fruit in the garden, God asked, "Where are you?"

The God of the Universe, the Maker of Heaven and Earth, the One who hung the stars in the sky, knew precisely where they were. God is all-knowing, all-powerful, and all-loving. He loves us unconditionally with a fierce love. God cares about our emotions and what we're feeling.

Questioning Adam and Eve about their location had nothing to do with where they were. Adam responded with fear, provoked by a realization of his nakedness, and hid in shame.

I didn't read anywhere about Adam needing or receiving glasses. So, what prompted this vision change? Perspective. "When Eve *saw* that it was good." Wait! *Saw?* Eve was looking at the *same* fruit in the garden all along, the same fruit she likely saw day after day. But suddenly, she saw what the enemy convinced her to see.

Through the pattern of repeated lies, the enemy convinced Eve to believe them, and she saw differently. She saw through the lens of pride and fear. Her alignment with God's vision of her was changed at this moment. Suddenly, she became a mirror image of pride and fear as she saw a reflection of everything she desired to gain and feared to lose.

Pride and fear often work together to cause chaos and take us off our purpose. Gone were rose-colored glasses replaced by the shame-filtered lens that entered the world — for suddenly, they "knew they were naked."

"Do not conform to the pattern of this world but be transformed by renewing your mind" (Romans 12:2, NIV).

One definition of a pattern is "an example for others to follow." For years, the media and diet culture have offered us their body image and self-image patterns. They fed their multi-billion-dollar industries instead of nourishing our health.

The God who sees us is offering us the nourishment of our souls and health through His Word. My prayer is that we fight and choose daily to make His Word our only mirror so we may reflect Him to the world.

Lisa Michelle Jones is an exercise physiologist, coach, Bible teacher, and founder of FITT By Design. Lisa champions women to find where they fit and get fit for their purpose. You may find her running miles along the Mississippi Gulf Coast's beaches, where she lives with her husband and four children.

My Marker Moment

Lisa Meiners

He was my baby. The one we had not expected but were then surprised by how complete our family of five was when he came.

As a baby of three in three years, he always wanted to be where his brother and sister were. Erik chased his siblings to the next stage of life — until he didn't. There was that season when he went on his path, leaving us deeply disappointed and, if I'm honest, concerned for his relationship with Jesus Christ. Although this season wasn't unexpected, it was unwanted.

These years were long as my younger son made decisions that did not reflect the training and guidance he had received for his first eighteen years. Not until he left our safe nest did I sense something was off.

How interesting is that? It wasn't until he left home that I wondered what he was up to. I could sense it in his tone when I called. I could read between the lack of lines when he texted, "I'm ok." I could tell from his disposition when he was home. And most of all, I knew it in my Momma-heart.

My youngest child has a fun-loving spirit and a sense of adventure and life. He brings humor and delightful orneriness to our family — without him, we would have been too serious. So, I chalked this season of my son's life up to restlessness or exploration.

He was on his own, with no one to answer to, no explanations needed for his comings and goings, and no one waiting for him at night. Erik was flirting with the very temptations of this world we had guarded against when he lived under our roof.

Each decision he made brought a natural consequence. And I'm so thankful for that. These natural consequences kept him safe. They were slow to come at first but quickly piled up: plummeting grades, leadership privileges lost, careless accidents, and job opportunities squandered. It seemed like the cycle would never stop.

Because I learned from my parents' example, I knew that lecturing and hovering were not our methods for corralling. Bringing him back to our safe nest wasn't an option for my husband and me. I was aware that the leash of parenting had been let out farther than ever before. Sensing something was off but not sure what to do, I prayed. Prayer was my go-to.

I prayed because my parents prayed for their three children every Monday. I prayed because that's what the parenting books tell you to do: pray every day for their path. If you don't pray for them, who will?

So, I prayed. But here's the kicker: I didn't just pray for those reasons; I prayed because I believed in prayer. I knew God was there. I wasn't sure what He would do with my younger son's actions.

Would God let Erik hit rock bottom? Would I even know from five hours away if he did? Would he lose his privilege to be in school? Would he lose his place on the sports team? I trusted God but didn't know how God would bring Erik to Himself in this unwanted season.

Mom used to say, "God can't be anything other than who His Word says He is."

God's Word says He hears, cares for, and knows me by name. So, I believed this for my son. I even reminded God that He knew how many hairs were on my son's head (Psalm 139). Did you catch that? I reminded God how intimately He knew Erik.

When we are hurting, and the unexpected takes over our normal, we remind God of what we think He might have forgotten. We speak His promises back to Him. It's either that or become incredibly angry, and that felt insubordinate. My heart hurt, my mind worried, and my tongue searched for explanations or advice that would snap him out of it. But I stayed humbly before my God.

When our loved one is wandering, we often look and listen for the perfect message or the put-together peer who might speak truth and wisdom into our loved one's life. We feel alone because the sheep has gone astray. We wonder if God hears our constant shouts up to Him—in the morning, at noontime, and as we close our eyes for another sleepless night.

Does He see our tears? Does He know our hurting hearts? Does He hear our incessant chatter, repeatedly asking for a rescue mission?

Then a moment happens. The sun breaks through the clouds on a random rainy day. In comes the very encouragement our soul cries out for at just the right time. A glimpse of what we believe is true: God sees and cares for our child.

Before the sun rose one day, I sat in my secret space, praying yet again, and my phone dinged. Because I was desperate for a word from the Lord more than the Word of the Lord, I grabbed my phone, hoping God was on the other end, bringing my aching heart relief from the suffocating wonder of my son's missteps.

My friend had been up early that morning praying. She didn't wake up to pray for my son. She doesn't even know my son. But God does. And she told me He put my son on her heart—my marker moment when El Roi, the God who sees, saw me.

I knew He saw me because this friend who just texted me didn't truly know me, but she knew God and was available to be used by Him. So, God used her faithfulness to let me know He saw me and heard my cries.

Even now, years later, my chin quivers as I remember that day. Tears threaten to drop onto my keyboard as my heart reengages with that moment. There's a lump nestled in my throat the size of a golf ball.

Do you know of a marker moment like this? A moment with no other explanation but God. Wow! The God of the universe, to whom I had surrendered my life and family, chose to answer me at that moment.

My friend's text read, "Don't worry about your son. God's got him. Trust God to have His way with him."

I sat stunned, awed, and overwhelmed. The presence of God was in my space. All I could give back to her was the smiling emoji with tender tears threatening to spill over.

She asked if he was struggling with troubles that made my heart anxious. She didn't have any idea what was happening. How could she? We had just started to become friends and had hardly spent time together.

I had barely shared about my family, and she knew little of my life and less about my kids. But at that moment, I knew God had seen me. I was confident He had heard every whispered or shouted prayer, every desperate cry for my son to return to the God of our faith.

God didn't see me in that moment because I'm a perfect daughter or a stellar servant in His name. I'm imperfect and can wrestle with God in the nighttime hours just as Jacob did. I can sometimes love my kids more than I love God. I can forget to be in the Word consistently. I can live in the joys of this world rather than trust in His love.

God loves you as He loves me. He sees each of us because we are His creation. He will involve Himself with our heart's cry because no situation is lost on Him. Every moment is His because He neither sleeps nor slumbers.

That early morning, I picked up my phone and knew God saw me. Just as His name states He will, for He cannot be anything other than what His Word teaches.

My son returned, but it wasn't that day. He still had some wandering, and I still had some trusting to do. But I knew God heard me and cared for my son beyond my deep love for him. Being seen by God is being known by your Creator, and being known by your Creator means He will tend to your cares.

El Roi holds Erik in the palm of His hand. He cares for him more than I can, so I rest in a posture of prayer. Even though Erik is responding wholeheartedly to God's pursuit of his life, another person needs me at Jesus' feet on their behalf. So, I pray, trusting in the God Who Sees, El Roi.

Lisa Meiners grew up in Lima, Ohio. She attended Nyack College and earned a degree in elementary education. She currently lives in Beavercreek, Ohio, with her husband Dennis. They have three children: Rachel (Gio), Kevin, and Erik. Lisa is an avid reader when she isn't writing, speaking, or teaching Bible studies.

Even in Winter

Angela Burtis

Imagine following a somewhat predictable and largely pleasant trajectory for your life when, without warning, stability and confidence are stripped by a painful loss. One minute, you know what you were created to do—and execute it with joy and intention. The next, you've lost your footing. What once was clear is difficult to discern in this new unwelcome climate.

My husband and I were happily married for over two decades, in the summer of our lives, busy raising three healthy and enjoyable teenagers, and drawing the most profound purpose from our local church in worship, service, and friendships. Scott was one of the pastors, and I led the women's ministry while working at our kids' school. We endured hard times—which come and go—but in the moment, we were fulfilled and seemed to be bearing much fruit for God's kingdom.

Eventually, sensing God's leadership, we accepted similar positions at a different church about ninety minutes from our home. Our kids embraced our enthusiasm, though their losses and adjustments were substantial. We said goodbye to our local family and dearest friends, excitedly expecting to bring our gifts and successes to a welcoming new faith community. The first few weeks were joyful and satisfying as we made new friendships and served together with ease.

Too soon, the wind changed. A toxic mixture of pride, insecurity, and blind allegiance in the church leadership assaulted us on all sides. Before ten months were complete, we found ourselves misrepresented, falsely accused, and slowly crippled, making any further contribution unfeasible. The shocking demise was painful. We didn't know then that we had just entered what I would later call our three-year winter.

What does a winter of the soul look like? For this stunned, wounded couple and our almost grown children, it looked like unemployment and underemployment. We met rejection at every attempted opportunity. No one wanted us. Suddenly disoriented and lonely, we searched for answers. Who are we without a solid church family to be assimilated into? Without jobs and steady income? What do we do now?

We confessed every sin imaginable and were more than willing to own any offenses we may have committed. Stripped of daily church ministry, we wondered what we did and why God seemingly put us on a shelf. Was He mad at us?

We waited for answers, any response. We prayed continually, asking God to use us again, for a church to love that would love us, and to give us another chance. Every morning, I scuffled to my favorite chair, where I habitually met with God to read the Bible and talk with Him. Once, this was my favorite part of the day; now, I sat shell-shocked and weary.

From experience, I knew God was with me and believed His promise to never leave me, but I couldn't feel Him or hear His voice. Most prayers were met with silence. Our circumstances didn't change for three long years.

With minor and sometimes no income, I recall only spending money on food, gas, mortgage, and utilities. We depended on God in every area of our lives. Living by faith, not by sight, took on a much more literal meaning when we couldn't see where our next paycheck or job would come from or when.

Winter is notorious for shorter days, longer nights, and frigid temperatures that drive us inside. Cloudy, gray days drag on with seemingly no end. Summer-lush vegetation withers and dies; nothing grows. The season yields lengthy sleep, and the sun is unavailable for early awakenings. If we let it, winter brings time to slow down the quicker, fair-weathered pace and succumb to the long season's rest.

Spiritual winter, too, is a decelerated season. Summer boasts bright, energetic, joy-inspired fun, but winter drags dim and feels like hard work. What once bloomed vibrantly now withers, dormant. Perhaps part of us must also die to make room for something new in the next season. For winter has its work to do. If there is no death, there is no new life.

We always have a choice about how we look at life. We prance with abandon—broad smiles and high fives—when all is right in the world and things are going the way we want them to. When the cold winds of pain and suffering blow, we also stand at a crossroads. We can resist, mourn the good old days, and beg God to make it stop. At the first sign of discomfort, we enlist friends to pray on our behalf for quick release.

Or we can fix our gaze on Jesus and His many promises to care for us lovingly, no matter the season. We can pray in faith as King Jehosophat did when he was headed into a sure military defeat, "For we are powerless. We do not know what to do, but our eyes are on you" (2 Chronicles 20:12).

My husband repeatedly asked God to show up, meet our needs, and surprise us with provisions we couldn't manufacture for ourselves. We dared Him to show off in ways that would cause our children and everyone watching to marvel at how our promise-keeping Father took care of us.

During my angst, well-meaning friends asked how I was getting through each day with no solutions on the horizon. My answer was a declaration, often in tears and on my knees, "Father, I don't know what You're doing or when

You will rescue us, but I am convinced You will. I trust You. I know You love us, and I refuse to doubt in the dark what I easily believed about You in the light."

In her most desperate moment of rejection, abuse, and fear of the future, Hagar was visited by God. As recorded in Genesis 16, the angel of the Lord found her and asked a few revealing questions: "Where have you come from, and where are you going?"

Hearing her perspective, He blessed her and her son and then returned them to the unchanged situation. Hagar's response to the angel has encouraged generations. She gave God a name to describe what she experienced in her conversation with Him.

Can we just pause in awe and wonder that this desperate woman was given a face-to-face encounter with the Lord?

"She gave this name to the Lord who spoke to her: 'You are the God who sees me,' for she said, 'I have now seen the One who sees me'" (Genesis 16:13, NIV).

El Roi: the God who sees me.

El Roi showed up on countless occasions during our winter. We received odd jobs, gift cards, checks, and cash in person or through the mail from friends, family, informed acquaintances, and our favorite, anonymous. One envelope read: "To Scott and Angela, From God."

The Lord saw us. He provided every need. He repeatedly demonstrated His love for us, usually at our lowest moments. He didn't change our situation or circumstance on our timetable because winter had to do its work in us—some things needed to die, like self-sufficiency, people pleasing, and pride. We had much to learn and experience about God that couldn't come any other way, like His provision, faithfulness, and commitment to us.

One proof that El Roi was watching over us was our timely awareness of Psalm 66, which propelled us to the finish line and the change of seasons. Desiring not to limp out of our winter battered and broken but rather strengthened and with robust gratitude, we clung to the words in Psalm 66:5–12 (NIV):

Come and see what God has done;
he is awesome in his deeds toward the children of man.
He turned the sea into dry land;
they passed through the river on foot.
There did we rejoice in him,
who rules by his might forever,
whose eyes keep watch on the nations –
(He) has kept our soul among the living
and has not let our feet slip.
For you, O God, have tested us;
you have tried us as silver is tried.
You brought us into the net;
you laid a crushing burden on our backs;
you let men ride over our heads;
we went through fire and through water;
yet you have brought us out to a place of abundance.

Eventually, the spring wind blew with gusto. With its arrival came new ministry assignments, new scenery in a move to the beautiful Adirondack Mountains, and a new group of people to love and serve with. And so much more.

A place of abundance cannot begin to describe the glorious exit from our three-year winter. El Roi always had His eye on us.

Angela Burtis is a pastor's wife with over twenty-five years of experience ministering and speaking to women. She is passionate about educating and challenging Christian women in every area of their faith with the question, "Is being transformed into the image of Christ the most important thing in your life?" Connect with her at AngelaBurtis.com.

Jesus Sees the Multitude,
Healing Many Who Came

Mike Velthouse

Read Matthew 8:16-17, Mark 1:32-34, Luke 4:40-42

As the sun began to set over the Mediterranean Sea on this Sabbath evening, people gathered outside the door of the most famous house in Capernaum. It had been quite a day, beginning that morning with Jesus healing a demon-possessed man in the synagogue, a powerful display of His authority over evil spirits.

Then, the scene shifted quickly to Peter's house, where Jesus healed Peter's mother-in-law from a life-threatening fever, demonstrating His power over physical ailments. As the sun set, the Sabbath was officially over, so people could walk to this house without fear that their steps would violate a Sabbath day's journey.

What began as a couple of people entering the house soon became a multitude of men, women, and children from Capernaum and surrounding towns swarming it, lining up along the street, waiting to enter. Mark described it as "all the city gathered together at the door" (Mark 1:33, KJV).

Can you picture the scene in your mind? In the line, there's a father from Chorazin, his arm around his blind son. Desperate. See a woman from down the street, hunched over by a disease in her spine. Hopeless. Notice a man from Bethsaida, unable to rid himself of the evil spirit inside him. Despairing. Here comes a group of men from Tabgha carrying their paralyzed friend. Defeated.

This multitude contained a variety of people with a host of different issues. But they all had one thing in common — a deep-rooted faith that the man inside that house could heal.

What was Jesus' reaction? "And he laid his hands on every one of them, and healed them" (Luke 4:40, KJV). Every one of them! What love for that multitude — the sick, diseased, and downcast!

But this is quite a common theme with Jesus, isn't it? Think of all the times we read of Jesus being with multitudes of people. In the gospels, the word "multitude" occurs 80 times in our English translation. It's another 18 times for the word "multitudes." Sometimes, the multitudes were there to hear Him preach. Sometimes, they were there looking for a miracle or just out of curiosity. But they always seemed to be around Jesus.

Reflect on Jesus' behavior around multitudes. Can you recall a time when Jesus was in a hurry with them? Can you remember when having that many people surrounding Him stressed Jesus out? Is there any record of Jesus ever turning anyone away?

Absolutely not. Jesus consistently showed care for His people and concern for their welfare. Jesus sees His people in need.

In other passages, we learn that Jesus had deep compassion for the multitudes because they were scattered, like sheep without a shepherd (Matthew 9:36). This compassion stems from the fact that they were the sheep God gave to Jesus. And Jesus would lay down His life for them (John 10).

What do you think resulted from this healing night at Peter's house in Capernaum? Those who came with faith in Christ no doubt had that faith strengthened and confirmed.

Isn't your faith strengthened and confirmed just by reading this account? Indeed, this experience made the multitude want to know more about Jesus, His identity, and His ministry. We read that the very next day, they "sought him, and came unto him, and stayed with him, that he should not depart from them" (Luke 4:42, KJV).

Consider your response. Do you actively seek Jesus in your daily life? Do you approach Him in prayer, desiring that He never departs from you? If so, take heart, for you are part of the most extraordinary multitude, the one that will dwell with Jesus in heaven for all eternity: "A great multitude, which no man could number, of all nations, and kindreds, and people, and tongues" (Revelation 7:9, KJV).

Mike Velthouse has published many articles for children in the magazine *Ignited By The Word*. His first book, *Journey Through the Psalms,* was released in June. Mike lives in West Michigan.

A Sparrow Seen

Katie Chew

I had just said goodbye to my husband, not knowing if I would see him again. This was our first experience with an overseas Army deployment, and there was a lot I didn't know. How would I take care of our five-month-old daughter all by myself? Would he miss every "first" of her life? Would we talk again? Unknowns piled up while tears slid down my face in concert with the rain hitting my windshield.

As fears swirled and questions rose, I cried to the God who sees and hears, "God, if you're truly in this, please show me that you see me."

Now, I won't get into the theology of asking for signs from God—but it is clear that's a place that holds tension in the Bible. On the one hand, Jesus says wicked and adulterous generations ask for signs and that only the sign of Jonah— He resurrected—will be given to them (Matthew 12:3941). That is certainly enough.

On the other hand, throughout the Bible, we see God showing up with signs and wonders as He reveals himself to people. Think Moses, Gideon, and Paul.

At this moment, however, twenty-three-year-old me wasn't thinking about theology. Twenty-three-year-old me was worried, wrecked, and worn out. I was a kid with a skinned-up knee, crying out to her dad, struggling to find him through the pain and the tears.

During my broken, heartfelt plea, a bird flew across my windshield. It wasn't a magnificent bird. It was rather ordinary and dull. Unimpressive. But I knew God had drawn my attention specifically to that bird.

Filled with frustration and arrogance, I scoffed. I mentally argued that a peacock would have been better — a bright bird with feathers fanned and a tremendous train rattling. Perhaps the "eyes" on the feathers could remind me that God sees me in all this. Bursting with lofty ideas, I was convinced that my style made more sense.

Elijah possibly felt the same. When God spoke to Elijah in the pit of his despair, God called him to a mountaintop. With the promise of God's presence, Elijah waited. God, however, wasn't in the massive signs of powerful gales, shattering earthquakes, or razing fire. He was in a gentle whisper (1 Kings 19:11–13).

That same whisper, the whisper of the Almighty God, Creator of all, who was and is and is to come, spoke to me in that moment. His Word, which is life and a shield, reverberated through my mind,

"Are not two sparrows sold for a penny? Yet, none of them will fall to the ground outside your Father's care. And even the very hairs of your head are all numbered. So don't be afraid; you are worth more than many sparrows" (Matthew 10:29–31, NIV).

His Word was both a whisper and an explosion at the same time. Our Father sees an unassuming, insignificant, paltry bird. Immediately humbled and encouraged, my tears turned to joy-filled laughter. He knew better than I. No peacock could compare to the symbol of that sparrow. He made the heavens and earth, yet He sees if a sparrow falls. How much more does He see me? How much more does He see you?

Perhaps you aren't facing the unknowns of a deployment, but we all face seasons filled with uncertainties. Jobs, schools, relationships, and circumstances beyond our control can create a strangling darkness. But, child of God, take heart for even the darkness is as light to Him (Psalm 139:12).

No chaos in your life can upend our unchanging God. No amount of darkness can extinguish the Light of the World. No plot twist in your story can take your Author by surprise. He knows. He sees. He cares.

As you read this, I pray you won't begin demanding signs. Instead, I pray that you start to recognize the presence of an all-seeing, all-knowing Father in every facet of your life. He may show himself miraculously or remain silent.

However He responds, know that your interpretation of His answer does not define Him. His ways are perfect, and He knows exactly what you need: a sign, a nudge, silence, conviction, or simply to wait.

As you walk with Him, His Holy Spirit will grow you more and more to recognize His faithfulness from the beginning of time and throughout every detail of your life — even when you don't see Him or His reply is not what you hoped.

Beloved, God is not far off. He is close to the brokenhearted and saves those crushed in spirit (Psalm 34:18). Seeing Hagar's sorrow over her son, He met her (Genesis 16). When the enslaved Israelites of Egypt groaned before Him, He saw, inclined His ear, heard, and sent Moses (Exodus 3:7). He spoke to Paul in a vision to encourage his ministry (1 Corinthians 18:9–11).

While I was crying on a Louisiana highway, He answered my whimper with a bird pointing to His Word. Wherever you are, you are not hidden from Him. He still sees. He still knows. He still cares. Weary soul, seen and cherished by the Most High God, take heart — for you are worth more than many sparrows.

Katie Chew is a disciple, wife, mother, and writer. When she isn't busy homeschooling her children or running the children's ministry at her church, she enjoys playing soccer with her kids, going to the theater, and baking.

The Thief Called Shame

Michelle Marie

Following the detailed instructions I'd read online, I entered through the side doors. Recognizing my destination was just up the steps and to my right, I paused momentarily. It wasn't that I'd changed my mind, but simply because I wanted to protect the unwitting folks inside from the wrath, should it fall upon me.

I turned to look outside and listened intently. No thunder. No lightning strikes. Perhaps this was going to be OK. I saw a coat check area filled with coats, telling me that the quiet calm I felt was not because the building was empty. Hanging my coat seemed too committing, so I proceeded to the sanctuary and quickly found a seat at the back, unnoticed.

This was the first Sunday service I'd attended in over thirty-five years. Of course, I still believed in God, but I didn't feel worthy of God, nor did I believe the people of God would accept me in their community.

I often recount the funny parts of the first few services I attended, like how I stumbled through them without knowing what I was supposed to do. The sit-and-stand part was easy enough—I could follow the lead of those around me.

I was a bit apprehensive about the absence of a kneeler, though. I quickly recognized that I was the only one whose right hand rose to complete the sign of the cross whenever the Trinity was mentioned. There were a few awkward "Greet your neighbors" before I realized that the handshake part of this ritual was uncertain for everyone due to the pandemic.

I haven't, however, told much about what was happening inside of me throughout those first few services I attended. Ironically, the sermon on that first day was the story of the angel Gabriel's visit to Mary, where she learned she'd carry a baby conceived out of wedlock.

Not only was this a significant change in how Mary thought her life with Joseph was to be, but a baby before marriage was highly controversial. It could change her life dramatically. I knew precisely how Mary must have felt then and as she progressed through her pregnancy. While I harbored many thoughts and feelings to deem myself unworthy of God's love, the shame of an unplanned pregnancy was the most significant stake in the ground, separating me from faith for more than thirty-five years.

As I continued attending services and listening intently to our pastor's weekly sermons, I was taken aback by how relevant they were to different situations in my life. It is tricky to explain, but my emotions were so intense during worship. I tried to hold back my tears, but often to no avail.

More clearly than anything, I remember an uncanny sense of peace that came over me in that sanctuary. God's comforting embrace, I assume, letting me know He was well pleased that I'd finally come home. That alone could have kept me coming back week after week.

As the people of this congregation greeted me, I felt some shame introducing myself, because I'd distanced myself from God for so long before these hard times brought me back. To my surprise, everyone was so welcoming and genuinely interested in getting to know me. With open arms, they made me a part of their caring community.

A year and a half later, I've found the opposite of what shame had me believing to be true; the more of my story I bring into the light, the more love and support I feel from this faith family that has embraced me so well. And that's precisely what I've been experiencing with God, too!

Part of me feels ripped off now that I know what shame robbed me of experiencing for all these years. Shame thrives in secrecy. It manifests and roots itself deeper and deeper in darkness. Through the journey to understand better how my mental health reached the point of crisis a couple of years ago, it's become clear that my crisis was fueled by some longstanding lies I believed.

My inability to cope with the grief I was feeling was just the tip of the iceberg. Within me were some deep-seated beliefs about my worth. I'd allowed others' actions to determine the value of who I was. I decided my sins were unforgivable and believed I needed to make up for them in other ways to be accepted by others.

Believing I was unlovable, I felt obliged to suffer from others' poor behavior to feel loved, even for a fleeting moment, resulting in more shame. This journey of discovery and understanding seems to be never-ending, as more lies seem to be uprooted — just as I have come to understand the one better.

Then came the anger on behalf of a younger me who can't help but wonder, "Where were the people in my life who should have been protecting me?"

And then, more questions. Why didn't they see me? Why didn't they help me? And what about God? Why did He allow such things to happen?

But God! I wasn't invisible to Him. He did see me, and He knew I needed Him.

"'You are the God who sees me,' for she said, 'I have now seen the One who sees me'" (Genesis 16:13, NIV).

As I look back now, reflecting with a fresh perspective, I can see all the places where He showed up throughout the years. It wasn't a matter of Him not being there; it was a case of my not paying attention to Him. God was right there with me all along, and He definitely saw me when I needed Him most.

God knew I was finally ready to be rescued and redeemed. He set in motion a sequence of events and coincidences that only He could conceive. When the grief brewing inside me was finding its way out of every crack it could find, He chose my boss, whom I had a lot of respect for, to be the one to point it out and suggest counseling.

Knowing that would be a tough sell, as I'd adamantly refused in the past, He prepared an obscure connection with a therapist whose website thoroughly explained therapy and what to expect. When I was brave, I wrote an inquiry email, but then hesitated when I realized she was a Christian therapist. God put the *send* button right where the *save and think about it* button should have been.

Even though that therapist was booking three months out and not taking new clients, He made sure she had a cancellation the next day and nudged her to get me in. It was all Him, and it didn't end there.

While the therapist upheld her promise to work with non-Christian clients in whatever way was comfortable for them, I think God took that as His challenge, sat back, and chuckled. He knew He'd led me to her for more than just counseling. She got to answer all my bizarre questions about what was showing up in my life.

God was relentless and wise. He knew exactly how to reach me. When I was ready for more, He led me to a church that couldn't have been more suitable for me. No one else could have ordered that face-to-face meeting with the pastor as I looked for Alpha information that wasn't where it was said to be. I wasn't sure what Alpha was—I just recalled my therapist saying Alpha would be good for me. It just so happened that on that day, the church announced they'd be running Alpha.

Without Him, it's doubtful I'd have chosen a church with a female pastor who took a particular interest in my faith journey. How blessed am I? She has nurtured and helped me grow immensely in faith, and she's become a wonderful friend who's made me feel more loved and valued than I have in a very long time.

God most certainly sees me as He's nudging me to use my struggles to help others find hope in Jesus. In addition to all He's done for me already, He's given me the time and resources to explore how I may use my gifts purposefully for His glory. I still have a lot of healing to do, and I'm sure that helping others will also enhance that journey.

The way God continually shows up in all aspects of my life with the most unbelievable and constant God-incidences, I know He's well pleased with my progress. I can only imagine how delighted He must be when He sees my eyes open wide and a grin from ear to ear each time I notice one of the funny ways He lets me know of His presence. I am in awe of what I'm feeling Him do in me, and I'm excited for what He has in store for me next.

Michelle Marie is a new Christian and new writer, inspired to share God's grace she's discovered through the therapist in whom she found hope and the pastor who's nurtured her faith story—her bookends! She writes the stories she needed to hear on her journey to the brink and back.

Holding Space: The Power of Being Present

Nancy Bouwens

The sterile smell of the hospital filled the air and burned my nose as I lay on the cold metal table, radiation zeroing in on the unwelcome intruder in my body. Tears slipped silently from my eyes, each one carrying a piece of my heart.

At that moment, surrounded by the hum of machines, bright lights, and faceless figures prodding at my broken and naked body, even though one of my best friends sat in yet another room waiting for me, I felt so lonely. I was exhausted and broken at the deepest part of my soul. I wanted to quit.

The cancer had rewritten my story, and I found myself center stage in a play I never auditioned for. I've always been the helper, the doer. But was I asking for and accepting help? That's a whole other skill set, one I was not prepared for but was forced to learn in the chaos of diagnosis and treatment.

There's vulnerability in being seen, really seen, when you're at your most raw and fragile. It's terrifying and beautiful all at once. Have you been there?

From the first moments of my diagnosis, God, in his infinite creativity, began to weave a tapestry of support around me, not with grand gestures but with a thousand tiny threads of love and grace.

Love perched beside me in uncomfortable chairs for hours during seemingly endless chemotherapy treatments. Love shaved my head when the time came, brought meals, and sent cards. Love told terrible jokes so we could laugh and ugly cry simultaneously!

These beautiful souls? They simply showed up. They became Jesus with skin on as they sat in the hard places with me.

Have you been there? That place where you're desperate to be seen—not as a problem to solve but as a person with a story? I needed someone to hold space for all of me—the fear, the disappointment, and yes, even my stubborn hope.

When we show up fully present and give the gift of ourselves, this becomes holy ground. In these places, fear meets love, and love wins every time.

I think this is what Jesus modeled for us. Not a distant, pristine holiness, but a roll-up-your-sleeves, sit-in-the-dirt-with-you kind of love. The kind that doesn't flinch at our mess but wades right in. He stepped directly into the path of the overlooked and made space for their unfiltered stories without judgment. At the well, He invited the Samaritan woman's story of shattered dreams out of the shadows. When He met the leper, He didn't pull back but stepped toward the one who felt vulnerable, exposed, and alone. Over and over, Jesus created space for presence more than religious clichés.

Friend, this is our calling, too. Just as Jesus met people in their messiest moments, we are invited to step into the lives of those around us. Presence is a gift we can all give. It doesn't require special skills or a fancy degree. It simply asks us to show up, listen without an agenda, and hold space for another's story.

It's saying "me too" in coffee shops and "I'm here" in waiting rooms. We are reminded to "Rejoice with those who rejoice, weep with those who weep" (Romans 12:15, CSB).

We have no better way to practice this than simply being present with someone in all the every day, challenging, messy, complicated, ordinary moments that make up life.

Love is not about having the right words. It's about showing up with arms and hearts wide open and simply choosing to be with another. It's sitting in silence when words fail or leaving a message that says, "I see you, and you matter."

When we practice the holy calling of presence, we become a safe place for celebration, sorrow, laughter, and tears. In those moments, we remind each other, "You don't have to walk this alone. I'm not going anywhere."

The gift of presence is priceless. If you have walked through a season of vulnerability in which you were unsure where you would be safe and whom you could be safe with, you know this to be true! The gift of presence declares to the world that they are not alone. Hard places are held by a love that will not let go, and we become brave witnesses to every story wrapped in Christ's unconditional love.

I invite you to look around. Who in your corner of the world needs to be seen? Whose story needs space to unfold? Take a deep breath. Step forward. Offer the gift of your presence! You become Jesus' hands and feet in those precious, sacred moments.

In a disconnected world in a million ways, your presence will be the bridge that heals wounds, brings hope, and changes lives—one moment at a time. I've seen firsthand how presence can turn hard places into sacred spaces. Now, it's your turn. Be brave. Your simple act of showing up in ordinary ways may be the lifeline someone is silently praying for.

Presence changes everything.

Nancy Bouwens is a writer, mindset coach for midlife women, and professional silver lining finder armed with curiosity and great coffee. This sunset-chasing, hospitality-loving guru navigates life's twists with panache! Her superpower? Inspiring others to embrace their God-given spark and live bravely, strongly, and courageously! Follow Nancy at The Intentional Life - www.nancybouwens.com

Her Name is Photini

Tika McCoy

There came a woman of Samaria to draw water.

John 4:7, NASB1995

Samaria, located in what is now Central Palestine, is a dry, rocky, parched desert city. As part of the Mediterranean climate region, it is no stranger to sweltering temperatures, especially at midday, when the sun is at its highest position in the sky. Without cloud cover, the sun's rays warm the desert sands and rocks, trapping the heat and producing unbearable temperatures.

Those who called Samaria home in biblical times avoided performing daily chores at midday. But on this day, one ventured out. The Bible tells us this woman risked the unhealthy temperatures to draw water at the sixth hour, the hottest hour of the day.

Why would a woman risk heat stroke to labor in the desert sun for water? Simple. Because of her past. Weighed down with shame, guilt, embarrassment, and isolation from her life circumstances, she preferred excruciating heat over encountering judgmental eyes and gossiping tongues.

The Bible only provides a high-level overview of her sexual immorality. This woman married and divorced five times and lived with a man who was not her husband. The story does not delve into the sordid details that led to her sinful life. Whatever the particulars, we know she went to great lengths to avoid others.

We imagine that this woman positioned her scarf to limit direct eye contact. On this particular day, with head bowed and shoulders hunched, she may have glanced in all directions before sneaking out her front door. Satisfied the coast was clear, she must have quickened her steps towards Jacob's well. Finally, at the outskirts of town, we imagine she spied the well in the distance and exhaled a satisfying breath, relieved that no one noticed her.

Or so she thought.

Although her daily routine never changed, this day would be like no other. Someone appeared to be sitting at the well. She squinted for a better view and then doubted what her eyes saw, thinking, *It has to be a mirage from the heat.*

No one would dare draw water this time of day. Using a corner of her scarf, the water bearer dabbed sweat from her cheeks, and then she heard a voice: "Give me a drink" (John 4:7 NASB).

She stared at a man sitting against the base of the well. Her eyes didn't deceive her! How could this be? She had taken every precaution to avoid the town's people, but there sat a man with a foreign accent who asked for water. Hot, tired, and confused, John 4:9 (NASB1995) records her response: "Therefore the Samaritan woman said to Him, 'How is it that You, being a Jew, ask me for a drink since I am a Samaritan woman?'"

He responded with a kind voice and offered her something called living water. His presence must have comforted her. The woman had probably rarely experienced kindness, and maybe no one had ever offered her anything. Daily treks to the well exhausted her. Yet, she accepted his generous gift. "Sir, give me this water so I will not be thirsty nor come here to draw" (John 4:15 NASB).

Then something miraculous happened.

This kind man whose presence comforted her told her everything she had done without judgment, disdain, or ridicule. Before this encounter, I imagine she went into hysterics at the slightest mention of her past, but something was special about this man. John 4:19 records the conclusion of their conversation: "The woman said to Him, 'I know that Messiah is coming (He who is called Christ). When that One comes, He will declare all things to us. Jesus said to her, I who speak to you am He'" (NASB 1955).

She dropped her water pot and ran back to town.

The woman shouted and exclaimed that the Messiah, the Christ, saw her! He did not see her as she saw herself. He did not see her as the world saw her. Christ saw her as His beloved daughter and offered her the greatest gift she ever received: salvation through Him. She shouted the good news to the same men who shamed her. "Come, see a man who told me all the things that I have done; this is not the Christ, is it?" (John 4:29 NASB).

The woman at the well had a life-changing encounter with Jesus. She was indeed a new creation in Christ. Her name is reportedly Photini. Scholars believe the Eastern Orthodox Church named her "enlightened one," which translates to Photini. Today, she is credited as being the first evangelist to share the good news of Jesus Christ. Scholars also believe the disciples baptized her.

Talk about a transformation! There are many commentary entries about her short encounter with Jesus. Everyone who reads her story has been touched in different ways.

For our purposes, I want you to think about two questions:

1. What would it mean to you to be seen by Jesus?
2. Would you share the good news of His salvation with the people who hurt, shamed, and belittled you?

As soon as Photini believed, she no longer felt guilt. She saw herself as Jesus saw her: a woman worthy of forgiveness and salvation. And she forgave the people who shunned her.

If you are weighed down with guilt and shame, read and meditate on John 4:7–27. Then, ask Jesus to allow you to see yourself as He sees you — worthy of forgiveness and salvation.

Tika McCoy finds joy in spending time with Jesus and delving deep into His word. Her Christian memoir, *Broken Clay: Finding Renewal in the Potter's Hands*, reflects her deep love for God, her dedication to helping others, and her unwavering belief in the power of faith and restoration.

Opportunity Amidst Doubt

Bethany Widmer

The eyes of the LORD are on the righteous, and His ears are attentive to their cry.

Psalm 34:15, NIV

I had butterflies in my stomach as the thoughts swirling in my mind rose above the chatter among the people around me. The group was relatively small, yet as they introduced themselves, all but one had quite the list of accomplishments in the writing and speaking world.

As I listened to them, anything I had done seemed insignificant and trivial in comparison. My friend, an established author and speaker, hosted the retreat and personally invited me, knowing my professional experience and believing I belonged.

She even prayed against such comparison during the opening prayer, yet here I was, starting this beautiful day feeling like a failure. I wrestled with my thoughts throughout the day and continued on my drive home; however, a moment caught my attention and created a spark within me. One of the women mentioned she was on the MOPS (Mothers of Preschoolers) speaking circuit.

MOPS greatly impacted my motherhood journey, and I even spoke to my former group a few times when our girls were young. The thought went through my mind that maybe I'm a better speaker than a writer. I hadn't spoken in a few years and had, instead, focused on writing. However, I

I wondered if I should contact MOPS groups in my area to see if they needed a speaker.

I decided to sort through these thoughts and feelings and pray. Typically, I share these ideas with my husband, but this time I kept everything to myself and didn't share it with anyone.

I met with my friend the following month, and she asked how I felt about the retreat. I confided in her about my struggle with comparison; she validated that we all feel that way sometimes, so she prayed against it.

I was still unsure about my writing and shared with her the thought that maybe I'm a better speaker than a writer, but I kept the other details to myself. She told me to pray about it and go with my heart. Truth be told, I thought about it, but I didn't pray about it.

One week from that meeting I received a random text from a friend telling me a MOPS group was looking for a speaker. She asked if she could give them my name. God was the only one who knew my desire to call a MOPS group. Despite my not talking to Him about it, He knew!

Oh, how He cares about the yearnings of our hearts. Not only did He open the door for me to speak at a MOPS group, but they chose a topic I am passionate about and have already spoken on in the past. He cares about the details.

I'm unsure where this will go, but I felt this particular event was created just for me. It was a reminder that God sees, knows, and has a plan and a purpose for our lives (Jeremiah 29:11–14).

Almighty Father, even when I have doubts and insecurities, you are right there with me. You see my struggles, and you answer my cries in a way that is best for me. Thank you for knowing me so personally and for caring about the deepest desires of my heart. In Jesus' name, I pray. Amen!

Bethany Widmer is a writer, speaker, and certified life coach. She has served in various ministries (children, women, marriage) since 1997. Her passion is supporting and encouraging others to pursue their God-given calling. She and her husband of nearly 30 years, Scott, have raised three daughters—Samantha, Emma and Sophia. www.bethanywidmer.com

Remember, Realize, Reach

Courtney Doyle

Do you ever find yourself sitting and wondering? I prefer to spend my wondering moments on a porch in the summer, tea in hand, rocking in a chair, listening to the birds sing and the wind blowing through the trees. I have always had a curious spirit, even more so about God and His presence in my life.

I wonder, did God see kindergarten me, sucking my thumb and clinging to the pant leg of the only caregiver I had ever known and loved?

Did God see sixth grade me, playing on the playground alone, longing to be included?

Was He aware of the constant bullying and name calling in high school?

Where was He the first time the man threatened me and followed through with his hands?

Was He there when I lay on the table making a life-altering decision?

Did God see me at all?

Did God see us as we fled the storm that left us homeless?

Did He see the heartbreak in caring for a child whose mother was incapable?

Where was He as I entered that prison to see my son's face on the other side of the glass wall?

Did God see me at all?

If you are like me, I bet you have wondered, *Does God see me, see us, see this?*

You may have lived your life knowing He saw, or you have tried to escape that reality or have believed He was keeping a record of your wrongs. You may be convinced if you're going through a difficult present state, that He is absent and is only seeing others around you.

Genesis 16 tells the story of a woman God saw, pursued, and redeemed. Hagar, an enslaved Egyptian slave-turned-mistress, would give birth to Abraham's first son, Ishmael, and would be rejected. Hagar ran from her life only to be found by the One. As she fled the abuse from Sarah, Hagar stopped for a drink of water and was found, seen, and her life transformed by El Roi, the God who saw her!

He asked two critical questions: "Where did you come from?" and "Where are you going?"

In our past lives, He saw us.

Luke 19 tells the story of Zacchaeus, the tax collector, a sinner, outcast, and thief. He wanted to see Jesus, and due to his short stature, he climbed a tree to glimpse this man the town was buzzing about. Jesus *saw* him. Jesus knew who he was, what he did, and what others thought of him, but He saw him anyway.

Jesus said to him, "Today salvation has come to this house, because this man, too, is a son of Abraham. For the Son of Man came to seek and save the lost" (Luke 19:9–10, NIV).

In our present lives, He sees us.

John 4 tells of a Samaritan woman at the well. Jesus asked her for a drink and began to tell the woman the details of her life that He had seen. His purpose in seeking her was to provide her with living water, not just the temporary thirst quencher from the well. He saw her, her past, her present, and her future.

The woman said, "I know that Messiah" (called Christ) "is
coming. When he comes, he will explain everything to us."
Then Jesus declared, "I, the one speaking to you — I am he" (John 4:25– 26, NIV).

In our future, He sees us.

The past is often a place we run from, where pain tells lies and memories haunt us. The past is exactly where El Roi was telling Hagar to return: "Where did you come from" (Genesis 16:8).

In the present, we stop, search for a better way, climb a tree to seek God, and determine which path to take.

The future is where we find our dreams, desires, and hope, "The Messiah is coming" (John 4:25).

From the Old Testament to the New Testament to today, I see a common theme as I sit at this computer writing to you. We all have a story. El Roi sees us, seeks us, and saves us. I would like to put a bow on that package and leave you feeling so loved and seen, but you are called to more. The God who sees, seeks, and saves also commissions.

"Then Jesus came to them and said, 'All authority in heaven and on earth has been given to me. Therefore, go and make disciples of all nations, baptizing them in the name of the Father, Son, and the Holy Spirit, and teaching them to obey everything I have commanded you. And surely I am with you to the very end of the age'" (Mathew 28:18–20, NIV).

Remember, your story matters.

Realize everyone has a story.

Reach into the lives of others.

Others may not flee their circumstances like Hagar and take the gospel to themselves.

Climb the tree with a friend who desperately needs Jesus.

Sit at the well with the hurting and show them how the Living Water can transform their lives.

El Roi is watching and longing for us to live as He intended, leading others to His arms so they know He is the God Who Sees.

Courtney Doyle is the creator of Courtney Doyle Ministries and Masquerade of Motherhood (The MOM Show) podcast. Basing her identity on the successes and failures of her children, she found herself teetering on a dangerous tightrope of pride and defeat. She is here to encourage you to find balance in the arms of Jesus. Contact Courtney: https://www.instagram.com/courtneydoyle_8/
https://www.facebook.com/courtneydoyleministries
or https://www.courtneydoyleministries.com/

God's Sky

Cara Shine

Think back to the last time you saw a real night sky. The kind that requires a long drive out of the city to where pavement becomes dirt, the haze of noise and light pollution disappears, and suddenly the stars look more like sand on a beach than the ones you can count. There's a stillness in the air, and the color black suddenly needs to be redefined because *this* shade seems other-worldly.

I remember the first time I saw an actual night sky. I was nine years old, and my parents sent me to Girl Scout camp. I remember our setting up our tents, cooking dinner over a campfire with our tin mess kits, and playing 1,000 games of red light and green light until our troop leader begged us for a rest.

Once the sun had set, our troop leader gathered us for a nighttime hike. We turned on our flashlights, held hands, and made the long trek out into a meadow. We walked, heads down, to avoid tripping on rocks or, worse yet, stepping on something gross, so we hardly noticed our beautiful surroundings.

Eventually, our scout leader halted our little procession and told us to get quiet, turn off our flashlights, and look up. The grass had a sweet, wet smell, and I heard frogs croaking from a nearby stream. Lightning bugs drifted all around us in the warm night air.

Our giggles and chatter subsided as our eyes adjusted to the darkness, and then we looked up, one by one.

I can still remember that moment. I heard tiny gasps coming from each of my friends and realized one of the gasps was mine. As the bigness of the night sky swept over our little hearts, I remember swaying a bit, afraid I might lose my balance as I tried to make sense of the sheer enormity of the night sky.

I was too young to name that feeling, but looking back now, I'm confident that was the first time I saw God. If I'd had the words back then, I would have asked, "God, can you see me, too?"

When God revealed himself to Abram for the first time, He also left Abram speechless by using the night sky.

"He took him outside and said, 'Look up at the sky and count the stars – if indeed you can count them.' Then he said to him, 'So shall your offspring be'" (Genesis 15:5, NIV).

And how did Abram respond to the magnitude of God's night sky?

"And he believed in the LORD, and he credited it to him for

righteousness" (Genesis 15:5, NIV).

Have you ever stopped to think about the first few paragraphs of the Bible? If you read closely, you'll see that God created everything on earth as evidence of His abounding love.

"In the beginning, God created the heavens and the earth"
(Genesis 1:1, NIV).

Then He created light, water and sky, land and sea, the stars, the sun, the moon, and finally, living creatures. His first blessings were all things we can see.

We'll have to wait until we are welcomed home to see God in person, but until that glorious day, we can look up at the night sky and know we are in the presence of our Father, who created all things for His good.

So tonight, if the sky is clear, go outside, look up, fall to your knees, and see all the evidence of God's love – because He sees you.

Cara Shine is a retired elementary school teacher with a passion for faith encouragement, anxiety management, and deep belly laughter. Cara is also a professional God Wink hunter. Her faith story, "Two Snipers, One Miracle," will reignite your passion, open your eyes to the lost, and remind you that God can turn ashes into beauty. You can contact her at www.Carashine.com

Complicated Grief

Kristi Lowe

When my mother passed, I learned that grief can be as complicated as relationships.

It was only natural that her passing would bring mixed emotions. Ours was a complicated relationship, but not for lack of love. She was not unlike a hurricane—fierce, strong, unapologetic, but also sometimes destructive. As for me, I suppose the nut did not fall far from the tree.

As a child, I reverently feared the woman who raised me. She stood six feet tall, a larger-than-life presence that filled every room she entered. Her laugh was contagious, and her lipstick was the brightest shade she could find. In the summer, she wore loud Hawaiian print dresses, had her bleached hair cropped short, and smelled like lilies and honeysuckle.

Her name was Betsy.

Betsy was the daughter of a WWII veteran who had survived a gunshot wound to the head while defending the northern border of Italy. Before anyone knew what PTSD. was, Betsy lived with it.

She came into motherhood broken, in an era that did not yet understand mental illness nor dare speak of such. As her firstborn child, behind closed doors, I saw a side of her few others did, tucked neatly away in public behind a mask of cheery brightness.

I loved her as I did; try as I might, I couldn't help her.

Her broken mind descended into madness during my adult years, and my heart broke as I watched mental illness steal the best of my mom and upend our family.

After she passed, I was caught off guard by the swirl of emotions inside. Grief is sneaky like that, isn't it? You'd think it would just be sadness. Maybe a little anger or denial mixed in. No one told me I might be relieved or even find a deep sense of peace in her passing.

I almost couldn't talk about it, fearing what others might think. And yet, it remained. After decades of turmoil, a quiet calm of peace sat beside my sadness and anger, as though she belonged there all along.

In grief, I learned one big truth: It's okay to feel more than one emotion about something *because God is big enough to hold all the emotions He so graciously gave us.*

One of the great mothers of the Bible is Hannah. Before she gave birth to her son Samuel, she experienced years of infertility. Grieved by her inability to conceive, year after year, Hannah begged the Lord to bless her with a child. That would cause most of us to despair, raise a fist at God, and yell, "Why me, God?" Yet in her grief, she continued to believe God saw her, that He knew the ache within her.

Talk about complicated grief.

Hannah ached. But Hannah also believed.

In times of grief, there's peace in knowing that *El Roi,* The God Who Sees, saw everything—*every moment*—all along the way. He sees the aching in our hearts, the messed up family dynamics, all of those painful decisions, and the times you gave everything you had but still came up short.

He knows relationships and grief can be complicated, but that's ok because He throws tenderness and compassion around like confetti. I'm thankful the Lord sees past the surface to the depths of our hearts. He sees your grief in its fullness—the shattered heart and those tears you cried in the shower (I feel you, sister). He sees your mixed feelings of relief and sadness as you realize that while they're no longer suffering, you'll never see them again on this side of heaven, and the dreams you held for your future are forever gone.

But the Lord sees your faithfulness, too. He sees the trust it takes to give him your fragile, hurting heart. He sees when you lift your hands in worship and the tears that slide down your face while you sing (seriously, I understand the tears. They come out of nowhere sometimes). Like Hannah, He sees when you keep returning to Him, believing Him, and trusting Him.

But friend, *here's the best part*: The God who sees, also sees your future. He already sees you on the other side of grief. He sees your heart, whole again, and the wounds healed.

Even if today is dark, even if your grief is complicated, even if you have more tears than laughter, and you can't imagine life any different than it is right now. Even if we can't see it, He does.

He's already there.

He is, after all, The God who Sees.

Kristi Lowe hosts the *Even If Podcast* and is president of Even If Media, LLC. She knows life rarely goes according to plan, family dynamics are complicated, and mental health is no joke. Kristi lives in Lubbock, Texas, with her family and rescue dogs. Follow her on IG @kristilowe or www.kristilowe.com.

Finiding Hope: El Roi in Infertility and Pregnancy Loss

Patti Schultz

Then she called the name of the Lord who spoke to her, You-Are-the-God-Who-Sees; for she said, "Have I also here seen Him who sees me?"

Genesis 16:13, NKJV

In the midst of her suffering, a woman came face to face with El Roi, the God Who Sees, as described in Genesis 16:13. God noticed her pain and offered her comfort and hope despite her feelings of aloneness and invisibility. Just as He saw the woman in the Bible, He sees you in your struggles with infertility and pregnancy loss. You are not alone.

Take comfort in knowing that we serve a God who sees us. El Roi, the God who sees, is intimately aware of your pain, your tears, and your yearning for a child. He understands your grief and your frustration. He is not distant or indifferent to your suffering but is present with you in the midst of it. He sees your heartache, and He understands the deep sting within your soul.

You are precious in His sight, and He longs to comfort you and give you hope in the midst of your struggles. He knows the deepest desires of your heart. Trust in His perfect timing and His never-ending love, believing that He has a purpose and a plan for your life, even if it may not align with your expectations. Be hopeful that He will turn your sorrow into joy.

Prayer: *Dear God, El Roi, who sees all, we humbly come before You today, burdened by the pain of infertility and pregnancy loss as we long for the gift of children. We pour out our hearts to You, knowing You understand our deepest desires. Despite feeling lost or broken, we find solace in the fact that You see us, know us, and love us deeply.*

We turn to You for comfort, recognizing that only You can satisfy the yearnings of our souls. We cling to the promise that You are near to the brokenhearted, and we seek endurance to face the challenges associated with infertility and loss.

Grant us peace in our hearts and hope in our spirits as we navigate this difficult journey. Give us the courage to lean on You, trusting in Your unwavering love. May Your grace and mercy sustain us as we wait on You, knowing that You are the God who sees and deeply cares for each one of us.

Give us strength to hold onto hope, even amid sorrow, and to trust in Your perfect timing. Help us remember that You are working all things together for our good, even when our dreams are slipping through our fingers.

Thank you, El Roi, for seeing us in our brokenness and loving us with everlasting love. May we find comfort and joy in Your presence as we journey through this season. In Jesus' name, we pray, Amen.

May you find solace in the arms of El Roi, the God who sees, and may His presence fill you with tranquility and hope amid your pain. You are not alone, for He is with you, always guiding you through the darkness toward a brighter tomorrow.

Trust in His unwavering love and His flawless design for your life, secure in the knowledge that He will always be there for you. Cling to hope, beloved, for El Roi sees and cherishes you beyond measure.

Three Self-Care Tips:

1. Find solace in prayer to connect with El Roi.

2. Journal thanksgiving for how El Roi has cared for you.
3. Make time for an activity that brings you joy, as He sees your efforts and values your well being.

Patti Schultz has her doctorate in education, and is a seasoned public school principal, professor, interpreter, teacher of the deaf, and mom to three boy miracles. Residing in Roscommon, Michigan, she treasures time with her multi-generational family. Patti's decade-long struggle with infertility and recurrent pregnancy loss has shaped her perspective on hope.

The Willful Water Girl

Carol Feil

It was my fault. Everywhere I looked, the plants, big and small, were suffering. I could see the droopy leaves hanging limp and lifeless. In the windy mountain area where I lived, it was my job to water the plants at my parents' landscape nursery. I was the water girl, and I messed up!

What I didn't mess up was getting to football games on time. I saw my job as a water girl as the road to fun. If I watered, I got paid. When I got paid, I had gas and food money so I could hang out with my friends, which, at sixteen, was a high priority in life.

Looking back, I know it was the goodness of God that allowed my first job to be one where others quickly saw evidence of my work. I couldn't bypass accountability and pretend I had done a better job than I had. Although I wouldn't say I liked being corrected, I certainly didn't like walking back through the nursery to rewater plants. I had spent too little time in the first place.

But God. He saw me. He loved me, and He knew me.

He saw my weakness: prioritizing myself over the job I signed up for. He loved me enough to show me I needed His character to permeate my life. Best of all, He never failed to pour into me through others.

Looking back on that experience, I recognized the evidence of God seeing, knowing, and loving His people, even this water girl, in personal ways.

He saw me as a young teenage girl, growing in my faith but struggling to balance priorities and preferences. He patiently guided me through the choices of both. He never once said, "I'm done with you."

He saw me as a 17-year-old girl, when I reprioritized my life. I wanted to walk in God's confidence and truth and share the hope within me always and anywhere. He saw me. He knew my enthusiasm and nurtured my heart for Him.

He saw me as a college girl, deeply disappointed by the circumstances that made me leave my dream school, only to return home and flounder about what would happen next. He was there through the tears, the questions, and the stumbling and fumbling that followed me.

He saw me as a 21-year-old, dating the man of my dreams, planning an idyllic future, knowing I would need God's love, wisdom, and comfort in the years ahead.

He saw me as a young wife packing up and moving far away with my little family to pursue a dream of full-time service to others, only to have doors closed at every turn after years of training and preparation.

He saw me as a young mom questioning what was next and waiting for it to become apparent. He never walked away as I moved forward, often numb and unsure. When I felt as dry as an under-watered tree, He listened as I probed. He didn't always answer my questions immediately, but my trust grew in the God who saw me at every step over time.

He saw me as a young mom embracing a season of motherhood that wasn't what or where I expected but was a remarkable time of gathering new friends as my kids grew. He knew I would need those friends, that circle, to lean on and learn from in the years ahead.

He saw me as a struggling mom incapacitated by a disease that slowed me to a crawl, leaning into those friends who gathered around and helped my family through. He saw me and cared for me.

He saw me as an in-between mom, reluctantly letting go of the hands that I had held so tightly. Hands that loosened their grip on me to hold onto hopes and dreams of their own. He saw and comforted me through the tearful transitions of motherhood.

He saw me as an older mom, learning too fast how to say a long goodbye as my mother slid into the darkness of dementia. He saw me. He sustained me. He gathered my tears. He calmed my fears and reminded me that my mom found truth and solace in a well-watered garden.

He saw me as a mom, a daughter, and a sister, navigating shifting family dynamics as my mother's life changed. He saw me, He saw my family, and He comforted us.

He saw me as a mom whose kids were growing in their independence, saying lots of good-bye-for-nows as I helped them pack and prepare for their next adventures and growth experience. Again, He gathered my tears, calmed my fears, and held my heart.

He saw me as a mom who was leaning in and learning, in every season, new character traits of the God who created me. Through it all, He saw, loved, and walked with me, revealing more about Himself through His Word.

He saw me as a mom struggling to juggle all the title's responsibilities. He saw me bend under comparison's weight. He saw me and reminded me I am fearfully and wonderfully made in His image.

He saw me as a mom welcoming my kids' spouses to the family, knowing that the time between hellos was getting longer as they developed their communities and experiences. He saw me, and He comforted me through worship and His Word.

He saw me as a mom, wracked by guilt for unfiltered words spoken in haste, causing rifts in relationships. He saw me. He reminded me He had already forgiven me. He stayed near me as I walked through the humble process of asking forgiveness from others. He saw me as I pursued reconciliation with those I had wounded with my words. He saw me, and He loved me. He did not let me go.

He sees me now as the mom of adults, with time to water, garden, and grow. He meets me in my garden and reminds me of the young water girl who moved too quickly through watering. The lesson from that failure to now is how important it is to nourish and soak my spiritual roots in the refreshing waters of His all-knowing love. He sees me, knows me with all my faults and frailties, and loves me still.

Like Hagar. After Sarah mistreated her, she ran away, yet was seen by God. Hagar's words still ring true: "'You are the God who sees me,' for she said, 'I have now seen the One who sees me'" (Genesis 16:13, NIV).

He is a faithful God. In every failure and faith step, He saw me. He saw me then and loved me enough to let me learn early and often the benefit of honesty with Him, giving me confidence in Him now. He is faithful to His character and His Word.

As the psalmist knew, I learned: "I lift up my eyes to the hills. From where does my help come? My help comes from the Lord, who made heaven and earth. He will not let your foot be moved; he who keeps you will not slumber" (Psalm 121:1–3, ESV).

I am so thankful He saw me, even though I did not water well all those years ago. I have experienced soaking my soul regularly in the truth of who He is and the comfort He gives, and it has made all the difference to this willing water girl.

Carol Feil loves saying aloud what women are quietly thinking. She is a writer, speaker, and cheerleader for women who struggle with guilt and comparison. Carol wants women to know they are seen, known, and loved by the God who created them, and knowing Him makes all the difference.

Don't Sweep Pain Under the Rug

Angela Driskell

Tap, tap, tap.

I could feel the therapist tapping my hands in rhythm as I tried to slow my breathing. I'd been here many times before, searching for a way out of a dark emotional pit.

The counselor believed this latest bout of depression was my breaking point from sweeping all my past trauma and pain under the rug. The mess manifested into panic, anxiety, and depression.

I wanted to feel better but questioned if that was even possible. The therapist told me to take another deep breath and picture a past traumatic time. I didn't want to relive any of the pain or feel alone again.

From the time I was four years old, I had faced various types of physical, emotional, and sexual abuse.

I often wondered how one person could endure this hardship and still live.

Sometimes, I wondered if I'd made it all up. Did I have an overactive imagination?

Was I looking for attention?

Why didn't I tell anyone and seek help sooner?

I lived in constant fear and struggled to trust anyone, especially men. I questioned my belief in God. Where was God when all these horrors happened to me? Why did He allow them to happen? Did He not see me, or did He just not care? Why would a loving God allow me to suffer so much?

I was raised Catholic and liked the idea of God, but I never knew Him personally. I wanted to believe He was all-powerful, in control, and worked things together for good, which made it much harder to understand why He let others harm me deeply.

So, I convinced myself that I must have attracted the trauma. After all, *I* was the common denominator in my story. If I was the problem, perhaps I wasn't worth saving. Maybe God forgot about me.

It had been a year since I had been raped and left on the street, battered, exposed, and all alone. It took me three months to tell anyone what had happened. Authorities told me I didn't come forward soon enough; it would only be my word against his. They advised me not to press charges, as I would likely face years of trials, only for him to be found not guilty for lack of evidence. I felt hopelessly alone.

Suicide seemed to be my only option to escape my pain. I told myself the world would be better without me, so I wrote a note and went to the same dark parking lot.

But God had other plans. I sat alone in the middle of the night and was about to end my life when I saw lights coming toward me. A police car pulled up, and the officer gently said my name. He told me he knew why I was there and what I planned to do. He asked if he could tell me a story.

The officer hadn't found out about his own daughter's rape until a year later when he read her suicide note. Like me, she returned to where it happened on the anniversary of her trauma, with a plan to end her life. No one was there to stop her.

He wished someone had been there for her. To let her know she was loved, to encourage her to choose life. The officer vowed to do whatever he could to be that person for any other victim by returning to the scene on the assault anniversary. I felt his grief and didn't want my family to experience this deep sorrow.

He made a particularly impactful statement: "If you go through with this, then you are letting him win. He may have taken the last year of your life, but you have the choice not to allow him to take the rest of it."

My heart was immediately moved. I would not let him win. I left with a fierce determination to not only live but to thrive. I'd overcome and prove that my past could no longer hurt me. Nothing and no one was going to hold me back.

Looking back, I realize I decided to live free from this agony, but I didn't know how to get rid of it. So, I lifted the rug of my life and simply swept the pain underneath. Again. I became reacquainted with God and determined to see Romans 8:28 come true: "We know that for those who love God, all things work together for good, for those who are

called according to his purpose" (ESV).

I wanted my past to help others. I would be joyful no matter what and see good come from all my pain. I put on a brave face and went through the Christian checklist items: attend church, read the Bible, memorize scripture, pray, and even go on mission trips.

Even though I looked like I had it all together, I still wrestled with the same doubts. Does God see me? Why did He allow me to go through so much trauma? Would He care enough to keep it from happening again? Deep down, I still didn't trust God.

Burying all the pain and sweeping the doubts under the rug became my way of life. I put on a happy face, but I was still hurting. Even though I attempted to hide my distress, the questions and pain never went away, and my feeling of being alone never ceased.

The idea of ending my life still lingered, but this time, the thought scared me. I knew God was real and wanted to believe He loved me. I was a Christian, so why was I struggling with depression, anxiety, and even thinking about suicide? I wanted to be free from the nightmares. But even after years passed since I had any physical or sexual trauma, the burden never stopped pulling me down.

The enemy of my soul sought to kill and destroy me, and I needed help to fight back. I knew that God was stronger and already won the war, but I still felt crushed, defeated, and surrounded by darkness. This battle felt different this time. I longed to stop hiding and to know the truth. To cling to God as my light in all circumstances. I was ready to stop managing the symptoms and break free from all the pain.

When I struggled in the past, it felt easier to focus on the current issue rather than uncover the problem. I would focus on fixing pain, insecurity, defeat, anxiety, loneliness, and fear with a temporary patch. But this time, God showed me I needed to remove the rug and expose what was underneath to clean it thoroughly. A cleansing was required, and Jesus was the only path to proper redemption.

So there I sat. I was reliving each trauma in extremely intensive therapy and trying to take deep breaths. And as I did, God opened my heart to the incredible reality.

I sat down and asked God the hard questions one by one. He faithfully showed me the answers.

When I felt all alone, God was there by my side. I could picture Him sitting right beside me, weeping. God not only saw me, but He felt my pain.

I finally realized the power of the cross, the burden He took on, and the pain Jesus endured. The pain I felt was confirmed, as was the pain He felt. The Bible says He cried to the Father on the cross, "My God, my God, why have you forsaken me."

God didn't abandon me or turn from me in those dark times. He was there with me, and He is there with you, too. He is with us always. He sees us at all times.

Friend, I know how hard it is to grasp why a good God would sit by when He has the power to prevent terrible things from happening. I have learned that I don't need to understand why things have happened, but instead, I need to rest in knowing He is always with me.

With time, I can see His presence in my trials and triumphs today. I can choose to have joy because I know who God is, and He loves me. I know I will still face tribulation in this world, but I can take heart because He is with me and knows me intimately.

God is my wonderful counselor; I can cry out to Him in all seasons. This is the journey I've been on, and if you find yourself on a similar journey, I pray that you confidently know that God also sees you. Just like He sees me, He sees you too. We are never alone. We can stop sweeping the pain under the rug. Instead, expose it to His light and let Him bring the healing we need to walk in freedom.

Angela Driskell lives in Indiana with her husband, Bryan, and their fur babies. She is passionate about shining her light and inspiring others to choose joy in all circumstances. Angela's professional background includes work as an EMT, firefighter, public education officer, senior advisor at Apple, photographer, and founder of Journey Websites. Website: AngelaDriskell.com; Facebook: Angela.Driskell; Instagram: Angela.Driskell.

I Wouldn't Say I Like Waiting

Michele Keith DeRolf

My porches are some of my favorite places to sit and listen. No music is playing, and no baseball game is on the radio. I only hear the chicken chatter, the distinct call of a bobwhite quail, or another airplane taking off or landing.

Until that unmistakable buzz, that's very familiar to me now. I hear that buzz above other things since I know what to listen for.

My hummingbirds. Yes. They're mine. They return to me because I take good care of them and wait for them to return each spring.

But the waiting? That's my least favorite part. Then, once they arrive, I wait for them to visit the porch on their daily journeys. I wouldn't say I like waiting. It's one of my least favorite things.

We wait for many things: our kids to grow up, a raise at work, the report from the doctor, the check to come in the mail, or a pie to bake. We wait for the change of seasons, our baseball team to play better, or a slow waiter to bring our drinks. We often become impatient in the waiting. We focus on everything we're unhappy about (even things that have nothing to do with what we're waiting for). This vicious cycle can take us out or pull us under.

The Bible gives us a long list of people who waited. Abraham was promised a son, and Isaac was born twenty-five years later. Joseph stayed in jail for thirteen years for a crime he didn't commit. Moses hung out in Egypt for eighty years before leading the Israelites out. David was chosen as the next king, but didn't take the throne for another fifteen years. It seemed God was up to something in His waiting and in our waiting.

I've often hoped or prayed for things that seemed good from my finite, human perspective. Indeed, God wants me to have a job that will help support me as a young mom. Right? How could that be bad? And I'm sure He would agree with my request for a negative result on my blood work.

We believe we understand so many things. Yet there's a tremendous opportunity with each passing day, the subsequent trial, and the coming storm. Waiting is not wasted. Maybe God wants to fine-tune an area of our life before He answers. Maybe some excavation of our heart is in order. Could it be that our mind isn't where it should be? I wouldn't want Him to give me something I'm bound to ruin.

While we're waiting, what are we doing? Do we drown out the silence with another project, binge on another television series, or pursue whatever other things will distract us? Or do we lean in? Listen. Try to hear what He's saying. Pour over scripture as if our life depends on it.

What about worship? Have you ever tried to worship through something? I mean, wholeheartedly worship. Some of the most awful times of my life have been transformed by deciding to worship in the waiting.

So much of our life is like shifting sand; changes come and go before we can hardly see what's happened. But God? He is unchanging. He's immovable. So, what if we worship instead of giving our energy and attention or waiting for the enemy?

As we shift our focus to worship, little miracles happen. First and foremost, with our eyes fixed on Jesus, our waiting is put in proper perspective. Next, we align ourselves with Him in our worship (to include thankfulness, etc.). This ultimately can result in being able to discern and hear from

Him. Just like when I'm sitting on the porch, waiting for my hummingbirds, I need to be attentive.

Waiting is often painful—literally and figuratively. We're waiting for children to get sober. We're waiting for the biopsy result and waiting for marriages to be healed and restored. We're waiting for the long overdue apology.

I'll be the last person to minimize the volume of waiting. Yet, it's in the waiting that I've done the most growing, learning, and trusting. In that tension, I find release. It's the place of sweet surrender to the One who knows the beginning from the end and all the waiting in between.

"I waited patiently for the LORD; he inclined to me and heard my cry" (Psalm 40:1, ESV).

Michele DeRolf is a med-surgery and critical care unit administrator who resides in Shelbyville, Ind. She enjoys her hobby farm with her husband, Kenny, and their dogs Ruger and Remington.

Good News and Hard Times

Marla Darius

It was such good news. After having four boys and then a four-year gap with a miscarriage, we were finally pregnant with our fifth baby. We had that nudge from God to trust Him for another child, but it took almost a year from the last miscarriage for this answered prayer.

We had been in our "new" house for over a year when we got the baby news, and my husband's home office was in the only empty bedroom. That room was transformed when we discovered this baby was a girl, and for the first time, we could decorate with pink. Hubby vacated his space to make room for the baby girl!

My husband owns his own company, which was only about three years old then. I noticed he was spending lots of time in the office and getting very little sleep. When I asked him about it, he stated he was trying to ramp things up for the business to help our growing family. After the baby's summer arrival, I was a bit concerned when he continued to work eighteen-plus hour days, but my husband explained it away as "needed time to grow his new company."

Shortly after Christmas that year, my husband fell apart emotionally. The undiagnosed darkness of depression, which hid behind workaholism, stress, and sleepless nights, was finally exposed to the light. He could hardly get up, eat, or participate in family activities. And remember, we then had a six-month-old, and the boys were five, seven, nine, and eleven years old.

This was not what we had planned or expected at this stage of parenting, business, or marriage. But when do things go according to my plans?

We sought medical and spiritual help. Over the next eighteen months, he was able to focus a bit more and keep the business afloat. My husband was transparent about his depression with his business employees (who were also friends), and he asked them for more help at work and with clients. I doubled my efforts to stretch the ever-elusive dollar with coupons, sales, and hand-me-down clothing while helping at church suppers (where our family could eat for free) to extend our food budget.

We saw God in the little things each day. For instance, when my husband was too tired to help with dinner, kids, or chores, I'd tuck a sleepy baby under his arm, and he caressed her fuzzy head as she gazed up at her daddy. This happened often; they still have the most excellent, sweet bond.

We explained depression to the kids, and they pitched in more with chores inside and outside the house. They worked hard at weeding for pay at the neighbors' or grandparents' houses to earn some spending money to help with sports clothing required for their school teams and to have extra fun money, too.

Despite everything being hard, we pulled together as a family to continue to have God at the center with daily family devotions, asked for prayer at church, and talked with each other often to keep the marriage intact.

Sometimes, the winds ramp back up in a storm, giving you a second lashing. This occurred four years later with the economic downturn and our struggling business. We had to let the employees go to keep the business afloat and then discovered they had been stealing from the company for over a year, unbeknownst to us, which had added to our financial strain.

This felt like a sucker punch while we were down with this depression battle, and it hurt that friends would do this to our family. We asked God, "Why? Why was all of this happening? Do you see me? Do you hear our prayers?"

I didn't audibly hear an answer, but I chose to believe that He was the same God who was there in the sunshine, the rainbows, the new baby, and the fun. His nature doesn't change, but our circumstances, moods, and situations do. We decided to cling to Him amid the many ups and downs. But over time, I felt worn down. Even with that centered knowledge of my faith in God and who He is, I began to doubt that He heard me.

I was a local leader in a community Bible study during these years. We met weekly as a leadership team of about twelve women before the study. I asked the team weekly for prayer and healing for my depressed hubby.

Over time, I felt like a prayer burden to the team, that none of the prayers were helping, and that nothing would ever change. I wondered if I should stop asking for healing and help. This depressed husband with a short temper and the daily family stress was my new life.

I began to drift from the feeling that God heard me. Sure, I still prayed. Yep, I still held devotion time with my children. And yes, I still attended church and Bible study, but I was feeling unseen, unheard, and uncared for.

One day, I was silently crying out to God, pleading for healing and that He'd change my new normal. I just wanted to feel that God cared, heard, and would help me.

Just days after this heartfelt cry, I was in the fellowship area at our church when a woman I knew slightly walked up to me and offered to make a meal for our family. I was stunned. I asked her, "Why are you offering this?"

She replied, "I felt God nudge me just to make a meal for your family. Could you use one?"

I couldn't even get out the words. I choked up. The tears ran down my face. I started to ugly-cry. What was happening? How did she know I needed help?

God, you *did* hear me! You *are* there. You *see me*. You *love me*. You care about little old me!

I said yes to the meal; I can recall this was a turning point in my *heart and hope!* It was just a meal but so much more than a meal. God let me feel His touch and love for my family and me. I felt renewed and decided that if God can do this, He can do anything. I felt my faith boosted.

My husband's battle with depression lasted seven years before he was miraculously healed at a prayer weekend with skilled prayer warriors, soaking in prayer and the touch of healing from our Lord. During our time of dark depression and stress, we struggled, but we also learned so much about each other, our faith, and our children. We were restored in knowing deep in our souls that we could weather any storm with Jesus.

The blessings we could finally see on the other side were that my husband and I learned to share more openly with each other from the heart, we clung to Jesus in a new way as time went on, and we modeled for our children that we have a God who is there with us and hears our prayers. He truly is the God who sees. He sees me. He sees you. And He lets us know that we are never forgotten.

Marla Darius is a speaker, author, photographer, and nurse with five grown children. She is a teacher/speaker/encourager to women and moms and has led Bible studies, parenting, and marriage ministries. When she has time, she loves to snap photos, plan fun outings, zip around in her little car, and dabble in home projects.

Heavenly Perspective

Nancy A. deCardenas

Then she called the name of the Lord who spoke to her,
You-Are-the-God-Who Sees; for she said,
"Have I also seen Him who sees me?"

Genesis 16:13, NKJV

In this passage, we find Hagar, an Egyptian maidservant of Abram and his wife, Sarai, fleeing from their presence, running into the wilderness. and feeling hopeless, alone, and in despair after being treated harshly by Sarai. Hagar was used as a surrogate after her mistress, Sarai, came up with a plan to fulfill God's promise that she and Abram would have a child.

Unfortunately, Sarai tried to manipulate her circumstances since she was past childbearing years. Her husband, Abram, agreed to the plan and had relations with the maidservant, Hagar. But God sees all. Proverbs 5:21 states: "For the ways of man are before the eyes of the Lord" (NKJV).

At this point, Hagar found herself in the desert in utter desperation. By God's compassion alone and divine intervention, she was addressed by the Angel of the Lord in the desert. He shared that she was indeed with a child and was to go back and submit to Sarai. "You are the God who sees," stated Hagar to the Lord. "Have I also seen Him who sees me?"

Have you ever been in utter desperation—maybe in a personal crisis, with no control over your surroundings or circumstances? We all may have experienced traumatizing events; for example, the loss of a loved one, an illness, a financial crisis, being persecuted for our faith, being disappointed, accused, betrayed, abandoned, and the list goes on. Maybe you committed a sin you thought was unforgivable. Thank God for our Heavenly Father who sees it all, El Roi.

I can relate strongly to Hagar's situation in a particular event in my life, which was one of my life's worst, intense, unsettling times! Instead of the desert, I was on a boat in the ocean on a beautiful summer day. My family and I had purchased a home in Florida on the Gulf. We were new in the area and were called to attend and serve at a local church.

We all headed out in our twenty-eight-foot boat towards a local place called the Sandbar. People anchor their boats, jump in the water, swim to the small beach area, have picnics, play catch with their dogs, walk, play, and swim with their children, and engage in all sorts of other outdoor activities. When we arrived in the boat, we found the location packed. We continued driving and found another little island called Anclote Key.

Anclote Key was just as beautiful, with clear water and a sandy beach. We told the kids, "Hey, you can just jump out here."

We didn't know why everyone was packed at the other little island, as this place looked the same. As soon as they jumped overboard and began to swim, we saw the current was very strong. They were all holding on to my little one. My husband secured the anchor.

A few minutes later, I saw a monstrous-looking shark come up right to the side of the boat. I watched my three boys and my oldest son's girlfriend wading in the water. I cried out to God, and I began to wave my arms. They could not hear me at this point. My husband was trying to lift the anchor so we could quickly drive to the kids, but it would not budge!

"Shoot it!" I screamed to my husband.

"I don't have a gun!" he replied. This shark was half the size of our boat. It was a great hammerhead shark — approximately 14 ft. long. I could not believe what we were going through. The adrenalin in my body was in full throttle. I told God, "I did not see my life ending this way."

Meanwhile, I was standing on the side of the boat, watching the shark. I was intensely conversing with God. "I don't believe you brought us to New Port Richey to serve in a ministry and to watch my kids get attacked by a shark! Lord, if this shark turns towards the kids, I'm jumping in and hitting it with the gaff (a long metal stick with a hook or barbed spear at the end that brings in large fish)." I continued praying, "God, direct this shark to head out to sea. Do not let it go to the right or left where it will find the kids."

I was so not in control of the dangerous circumstances, and I was not about to see my kids get attacked.

I was frenzy and screamed to my husband, "Get a bang stick!" My dad always had one stored away on his boat when I was growing up going on fishing trips with him. My husband shouted, "I don't have a bang stick."

At this moment, I thought, *God is not alarmed; He is not panicking.*

God in heaven knew we would be caught up in this circumstance. God meets us where we are. "God is a very present help in times of trouble" (Psalm 46:1, NJKV) reminds us.

We witnessed with our own eyes in that beautiful, clear water that the shark swam straight out to sea away from the boat and the kids. A few minutes later, we were able to break the anchor free from entanglement or the hold of the ocean floor, and we immediately circled to meet and pick up the kids.

The kids commented, "We knew something was wrong. Mom was waving at us, but we couldn't hear what she was saying."

Then they all had to laugh at me because they noticed the gaff I was holding had a rubber cover over the hook, so it would not have done any damage to the shark! A few days later, we watched aerial footage of a great hammerhead shark, a fourteen-footer, patrolling the same waters on the Tampa Bay news. We became aware the current is much stronger throughout that channel, making it not a relaxing area to swim in. I had prayed, "My God! I cannot thank you enough."

Some residents in the area we spoke to afterward said, "Oh, yeah, that's where all the sharks hang out. You cannot swim over there."

I wished someone would have warned us, but I'm glad for heaven's perspective — the God Who Sees — He had us in the palm of His hand.

The God Who Sees looked down at us, His children, from His dwelling place, like He did for Hagar when she was endangered in the desert. The Lord saw her and made Himself known. That beautiful summer day on the boat, as the God Who Sees watched over us, I believe we experienced a direct answer to prayer when we saw that shark head straight out to sea.

I appreciate my family even more; I have more joy and personal introspection. What's most important? Our relationship with God and our relationships with others. Glory Be to God alone! We remained safe in a potentially dangerous situation. Amid a chaotic situation, the God Who Sees showered His grace upon us as a family.

Nancy A. deCardenas, author and speaker, received her B.A. in Spanish, and served in missions, women's, and children's ministries. She enjoys writing by Cedar Creek Lake. Her Devotional coming soon is *A Daily Word By Grace.*

What Do You See?

Pearl Manasseh

For the Lord sees not as man sees; for man looks at the outward appearance, but the Lord looks at the heart.

1 Samuel 16:7, Amplified Bible

Do you remember those games in books where a drawn outline of a simple picture, at first glance, might appear to be one thing—but could also be something else? For example, a pair of vases could be viewed as profiles of two people facing each other.

Isn't that a straightforward analogy of how we can perceive people, situations, religion, or Christianity differently, too?

Ronnie James Dio was a rock singer who died a few years ago due to stomach cancer. Many considered him a Satanist.

Before becoming a solo artist, he replaced Ozzy Osbourne as lead singer in the band Black Sabbath. During his tenure as part of Sabbath, he wrote a tune called "Heaven and Hell," one of my favorites for many years.

It's a dark song about the dichotomy of perspectives on religion and our choices. Essentially, it's up to us to choose whether we follow, without question, the dictates of particular harsh religious ones who only see sin and tell people (other than themselves, of course) why they're going to hell. Or do we ask questions, think for ourselves, and see the truth of what God and religion are supposed to be — love with moral standards?

The opening lines of the song reference the extremes of how others perceive its writer. Is he a musician who brings his truth and empathy into the world — or a sinner because he does it in a way that differs from what some think he should?

Dio is credited with creating the hand signal of a fist with the index and pinky fingers extended.

Some see it as the horns of Satan; others, a sign language symbol of love or acceptance.

What do you see?

Would it help if I told you he didn't do drugs, was loyal to his wife, and was considered one of the most excellent guys in rock? And in 1988, long before most people cared or even knew about it, he received The Children of the Night Philanthropist Award.

Children of the Night is an organization that rescues children from sex trafficking and gives them a safe place to heal.

What do you see now? Or maybe the better question is, *who* do you see?

He frequently wore black and some heavy metal jewelry, was a short guy with a voice that was soft when speaking and powerful when singing, had unapologetic opinions, thinned long hair, and was known to don a long black leather duster.

I still see a hero and a Christian.

None of us mortals will ever be perfect, and *all* are sometimes considered sinners and hypocrites. It's up to us whether we deem others should be kept out of church or Heaven or be grateful that grace applies to *all*, including ourselves.

In reality, it's only up to us to decide where we'll spend eternity — simply by choosing Jesus Christ as our Savior and Redeemer.

Dear Heavenly Omni-Everything-Including-And-Especially-Love Abba,

Thank You that You can see past our outer trappings and situations and into our hearts — even if what's in our hearts isn't always something to be proud of.

Thank You that You know our mortal frailty. Thank You that because we say yes to You, we can live in faith and peace, knowing where we'll spend eternity, knowing no one else can take that away from us,

Amen!

Pearl Manasseh is one of God's beloved daughters and has survived child sex trafficking, child sexually abusive material, and an abusive marriage. Her purposes include reminding overcomers that God is for them, and who they are in Him, via her blog *Pearl, Unchained,* talks, and human trafficking awareness events her nonprofit organizes.

God's View of Women

Denise Renken

I remain fascinated by the story of the woman at the well in John 4. During one Sunday service at my church, the pastor led his sermon on this Scripture by stating, "The woman at the well was the first person to whom Jesus identified himself."

I melted into the pew. The remainder of the sermon floated into the background as my mind paused. I wondered, "What did this declaration denote for women?"

The story begins with Jesus taking the shortcut to Galilee through Samaria. Although the shortest route, it represented the least desirable path for a Jew. Yet, Jesus had a plan.

To say Samaritans and Jews were enemies is an understatement. The Jews considered Samaritans something to be scraped off the bottom of their sandals. Many years earlier, the Jewish people had been exiled to the region, and a remnant of Jews remained there, intermarrying with the Samaritans. The merging of cultures created a spattering of half-Samaritan and half-Jewish people.

This segment of Samaritans embraced the first five books of the Torah, referred to as the Books of Moses. These books represent the first five books of our Bible. Their religion was an awkward blend of those books and lingering pagan worship. However, because of the Jewish influence, Samaritans were aware of the foretold Messiah and eager for His arrival.

Back to our woman. To appreciate what happened between Jesus and the unnamed Samaritan woman, it is essential to try to understand her. I imagine her beauty as breathtaking. She had been married five times and was living with yet another man. Indeed men found her attractive. Our woman chose the scorching heat of the day to visit the well. Only then could she avoid the scorn of other women.

Isn't it interesting that our cultures and base natures refuse to change even to this day? Unfortunately, some of us share snide remarks about women we find more attractive than ourselves. Layer on socially inappropriate behavior and whispers among women often run amuck. Sadly, in my twenties, I was among these whispering women.

This day was just another drudgery-filled day as she went to the well. She had no idea she was about to encounter Jesus. He had sent his disciples to Samaria for food. I can't help but wonder why Jesus did not ask *any* of the disciples to stay and rest there with Him. Perhaps He needed their potential interruptions from the conversation He was to have with her.

Unchaperoned, He began speaking to her. This was scandalous behavior, indeed, in this society. He told her to draw water for Him from her vessel. Buckets were not left at the well. He chooses to place himself and her in an awkward position. He was about to drink from a vessel provided by this harlot of a woman.

The inappropriateness continued. With her mind reeling with disbelief (in today's terms, she was inwardly freaking out), the conversation progressed as He told her of water giving eternal life and how He could provide her with this living water. Side note: the phrase *living water* is used in the Old and the New Testament to indicate God's gift of salvation (Jeremiah 17:3, Zachariah 14:8–9, Psalm 36:9; Isaiah 55:1).

Jesus then told her to go and get her husband. She told Jesus she had no husband. Here's what sent her mind racing—Jesus affirmed her statement as truth. He continued by telling her He knew her history of five husbands and her current living status with a man. They exchange more words, climaxing in verse 26, where Jesus says to her, "I who speak to you am he."

Few women were educated during this time. However, she and other women knew a Messiah was coming. The foretold Messiah would be all-knowing, including knowing *all* secrets. I think she mentally began to connect the dots. The man in front of her was the Messiah. I don't know how she was able to make her feet move.

In the remaining verses, the disciples showed up with the food, and the woman rushed to get other Samaritans so they could quiz Jesus. The Samaritans agreed He was the long-awaited Messiah, leading to the early converts of Samaria and salvation.

Three years later, Christ died on the cross, rose from the grave, and was witnessed as alive by multitudes. Before His sacrifice, the Samaritans were already believers in the deity of Jesus. All of this is extraordinary; everything Jesus did was extraordinary.

What is astonishing is that Jesus could have chosen anyone to reveal His deity to. Yet, He chose a woman. And not just any woman, but a woman shunned for a lifetime of sinful choices.

We are important to God. Satan whispers, "You are insignificant; you've done too many sinful acts; you are worthless." God whispers, "There has never been anyone and will never be anyone I love more than you. Not Moses, not King David, not Abraham."

Women matter to God. He sees us, catches our tears, and bathes us in His grace and forgiveness.

We are all women at the well, each bringing our trainload of sins to the altar. To think our sins are somehow less than hers is absurd to God. Thankfully, we have a Savior in Jesus. He paid the sacrifice of death as a penalty for our sins, allowing us to stand on the throne of God, innocent and pure. Jesus took our sins upon His shoulders.

Sometimes, we feel that all we've done, all we left undone, or all the things done to us make us somehow undeserving. God whispers, "You are my woman at the well, and I love you."

My prayer is to remember that I am the woman at the well.

Denise Renken, a mentor to women for thirty-five years, inspires women to experience the love of God. An author and speaker, she shares her testimony across the nation. She is a group president of Word Weavers International and a member of the Advanced Writers and Speakers Association.

When God Calls Your Name

Kelly Hall

*But now thus says the LORD, he who created you, O Jacob, he
who formed you, O Israel: "Fear not, for I have redeemed you;
I have called you by name, you are mine"*

Isaiah 43:1, ESV

Bundled against the freezing Midwest dreariness, I burst
into my house and collapsed onto the couch without
removing a single item of wintry protection. The wet, snowy
trail I left behind typically would have prompted a quick
flurry of activity to dry and protect the hardwood floors, but
today, I barely noticed.

I had moved halfway across the country with my four
young children so our three daughters, born with profound
hearing loss, could undergo surgery to receive cochlear
implants and attend a school where they would be trained to
speak. My husband, a fighter pilot in the Air Force, had
managed to secure a one-year assignment about six hours
away so he could join us on weekends.

Although we were starting to see significant benefits
from the school, I was overwhelmed with the daily demands
of parenting and facilitating communication between our
four "littles." But what surprised me was the pain of
loneliness. Adjusting to an unfamiliar city without the
nearby support of family, friends, military community, or
church home was more complicated than I expected. Never
had I felt entirely so unseen and unknown.

My inner turmoil spilled out in prayer. "Lord, thank you for leading us to where our girls finally get the help they need. I'm grateful for Your presence and care. But, Lord, my heart aches to talk to a physical person. Please send someone who can understand, who won't feel burdened by our story or feel they must travel across the country to help."

After skimming through a list of names, I gave up and told the Lord, "If you want someone to call me, You'll have to figure it out."

My phone rang as I prepared to drive to a nearby bakery for comfort food. A woman from a recently visited church explained the reason for her call: "For three days, God's whispered your name, telling me to call you, but I kept putting Him off because I didn't know how to help. But today, when He started shouting your name, I could no longer ignore Him."

This dear older woman had four grown children, three deaf. Her husband had been in the military, and they had moved to this same city for the same reasons we had. God sent me a precious new friend who could understand our complicated story. The wisdom, insight, prayers, and laughter that flowed through the phone were a healing balm to my heart.

After I hung up, I fell to my knees, stunned by this extravagant outpouring of God's intimate care. "Lord, I can't believe You love me enough to arrange a phone call from the right person at just the right time. You started orchestrating it three days earlier because You knew precisely how long it would take!"

My friend never could have imagined how her one simple act of obedience would become my favorite memory of God's faithfulness and love.

The Bible reminds us when the overwhelming challenges of life make us feel isolated, we don't have to be afraid, for the Lord knows our names. The One who created us, who formed us, who redeemed us, is deeply invested in our stories (Isaiah 43:1). His fingerprints are on our very souls (Psalm 139:14). Our names are inscribed on His hands and His heart (Isaiah 49:16). Before a word is on our tongue, the Lord knows (Psalm 139:4). Before our needs arise, He has positioned the perfect provisions (Matthew 6:8). What a comfort to know we are seen and know by our God, who is not only immensely powerful but also intensely personal.

Kelly is a podcaster, speaker, author, and passionate Bible teacher. Her *Unshakable Hope Podcast,* Where Real Life Intersects Redeeming Love, addresses the question: "How do we trust God's heart when His ways and delays break ours?" For hope-filled resources, visit www.KellyHall.org.

Just Give It!

Ann Yarrow

I could see him from the corner of my eye as I waited for the stoplight to turn green. He sat shivering on a bench, rocking back and forth, wrapped in a thin blue blanket. I didn't know him or his story, but I kept thinking, "That is someone's son," and I had compassion for him.

I asked God, "What can I do?" then it hit me, "*Oh . . . wow . . . God . . . that is a huge ask.*" I drove home, ran up the stairs to a vacant room and pushed my way into a virtual time capsule. Memories instantly beckoned me to sit for a while and brood, but I refused. I just wanted to help someone and not feel sad for once. With my hand on the closet door, I said out loud, "God, do you hear me? I am going to do it!" I wanted to make sure He knew that I meant business. This was going to take courage. I opened the door; my eyes rested on a heavy-duty black Carhart. I took the coat from its hanger. It was a sturdy coat chosen for one who loved the outdoors. My heart ached as I lifted it to my face and buried my nose deep into the fabric. His scent was gone. I knew it would be. It had been two years since he lost his life in a hiking accident in the mountains of Montana.

I stared at my son's coat. It had been on many adventures. No doubt this thing held some stories — chopping wood with his dad, walking the riverbank looking for arrowheads, hiking with his sister, wilderness camping with his brother, or sitting around a fire with friends. It was also the coat my husband and I had left on its hanger the day we started going through his room. So now it hung in a closet, not serving anyone. And still, we had not finished the job of boxing and sealing up his things. Everything we touched held a memory. It seemed we could never find the time to do a job no parent should *ever* have to do.

My mind returned to the man shivering at the bus stop, so with quick determination, I scooped up the coat, ran down to the car, and sped to the bus stop. He was still sitting on the cold metal bench, wrapped in the thin blanket. As I gingerly stepped toward him, I could see that he was hunched over a piece of paper, writing something. He wore a T-shirt and a pair of shorts. His dirty feet were jittery in his flip-flops, and his odor told me it'd been a while since he'd been able to bathe.

"Excuse me, sir?"

. . . . silence . .

Louder this time. "Excuse me, sir? I have a coat, if you would like it?"

I clutched the heavy fabric to my chest; memories of Josh and me in the woods quietly identifying songbirds flooded my mind. When he was very small, he studied and categorized animals. He was seven when our family went to the Grand Canyon. During a hike, he ran ahead. When we caught up, we found him giving a lecture on Mountain Jays versus common Blue Jays to a small group of adults. He loved to share his knowledge. He was always . . .

"No, I'm fine!"

The sharp tone of the man on the bench yanked me back to the present. "Are — are you sure? You look cold." I thought about the weather forecast and wondered if he knew what was coming. Exasperated, he replied, *"OK, give it. I'll put it in my bag!"*

I was stunned at his abruptness. My mind went blank, and instead of apologizing for bothering him and leaving, I handed over my son's coat. He opened his bag and shoved it in. He didn't *even look at it;* He returned to his paper. I slowly turned to walk away, and he mumbled something. I stopped and stepped back, "Excuse me?" I said, thinking he had thanked me. But instead, with much exasperation, he replied, "*I said . . .I put it in my bag!*" My brain went numb. No thought came to my mind. I couldn't have reacted if I had wanted to. I quickly returned to my car, shut the door, and immediately fell apart. The numb feeling I had was suddenly replaced by a massive boulder that had been shoved deep into my chest, ripping through my flesh and mangling my heart. *I felt duped. I felt taken for granted; I felt dumb, misinformed, and mistaken. "God? Did I hear you right? What WAS that?"*

Hot tears blurred my vision and streaked my cheeks as I drove home. I tried to understand where I had gone wrong. I sat at the kitchen table and laid my head on its cool, hard surface. I sobbed and asked God how He could ask me to give up something *so precious* to someone *so ungrateful*, to someone *so indifferent*. Had I misinterpreted God's leading, had I misunderstood? I felt so stupid. This man hadn't asked for help, he hadn't asked for a coat, and *who was I?* Some bored, middle-aged woman coming to save the day? But that was not my heart. My heart had been sincere; I wanted to obey even though I knew it would be difficult. Still, my brain kept rolling through all that had gone wrong. I thought about how I made this decision by myself. Would my husband be upset? He had no choice in what to do with his son's coat. I just did it. I had also assumed that this man wanted help. I began to think that God was toying with me.

Where was the affirmation of a job well done? The rush of joy? The increased faith? The payoff? I started thinking about the coat. I felt as if I'd handed over part of my son — memories attached and all. *"God, do you even see me?"* *"Do you have any idea how I feel?"* *"Do you understand what I gave away?"* My faith dove into a spiral. I was scared, "God, please help me," I begged.

Staring at the empty hanger, it struck me . . . I gave up a coat, but God gave His love. His love was sacrificial. It was costly. He gave His only son to a world that He deeply loved. He knowingly gave His son to those who would accept and follow Him with all their heart, as well as to those who would ultimately reject Him. He knew this even as the nails tore through his flesh.

What's more, He gives us good gifts every day! He gives gifts that I sometimes take for granted, like a sunny day, the beauty of creation, and food that I don't have to hunt down and drag home, at least not in the real sense. He gives the gifts of mercy, grace, compassion, and wisdom. I can be indifferent about such blessings. I don't always thank Him. Sometimes, I don't even acknowledge Him. I may as well say, "*Okay, give it, I'll put it in my bag!*"

But was this my takeaway? My payoff? If it had been easier, maybe I wouldn't understand the heart of sacrificial giving. I also realized that my obedience was not about the payoff. I can trust, obey, and wait on the Lord, whether I understand or not. Maybe, one day, I will know if my obedience in this life ever set off a chain reaction of blessing in others, but for now, I am blessed and humbled. I am grateful to God for giving His son, Jesus, the most precious and sacrificial gift ever. And as for the coat? Giving it away did not dull or take away the beautiful memories. I still have them. And God did see me that day, but in a way I did not expect. He reminded me how much He loved me and the rest of the world. He gave me perspective. He allowed me to trust and not always have to understand the outcome.

Ephesians 1:7-8 (TPT) says this, "Since we are now joined to Christ, we have been given the treasures of redemption by his blood—the total cancellation of our sins—all because of the cascading riches of his grace. This superabundant grace is already powerfully working in us, releasing all forms of wisdom and practical understanding."

And Romans 5:8 (NIV) puts it this way, "But God demonstrates his own love for us in this: While we were still sinners, Christ died for us.`

Ann is a Co-Founder of Get-Out-There Ventures, wife and mother of three, her youngest now in heaven. Ann shares her writing and photography on Ann Yarrow.com

God's Business

Kim Cusimano

Waterfalls and willow trees,
Sandy beaches and summer peaches,
June bugs and falling stars,
Sickness and disease.

God knows His why,
For all of it.
Light and dark,
Sweet and sour,
Hellos and goodbyes.

The world wants to be great.
Who can be —
The one with the questions
Or the answers?

I would do well,

To bow my knee.
Rest in peace, rather than greatness

Knowing He knows.

Knowing He sees.

The burden is in having a reason for stinging bees,

gusty wind, and raging seas.

It's God's business if He wants blinding blizzards,

Or thistle weeds.

It's more fact than possibility,

I only see a part when He sees the whole.

So if He wants to dress roses in thorns,

Or let the sun kill snow,

He is not accountable to me.

Kim Cusimano is a collaborative author. She finds joy and an expanded ministry reach through collaborative writing. As a mother to two special needs adults, she is passionate about encouraging people of all abilities. This passion influences her writing, providing readers with generous amounts of encouragement. Visit Kim at Fulljoyministries.com

Living Parables of Central Florida, of which EABooks Publishing is a division, supports Christian charities providing for the needs of their communities. Ministries are encouraged to join hands and hearts with like-minded charities to better meet unmet needs in their communities.

Mission Statement

To empower start up, nonprofit organizations financially, spiritually, and with sound business knowledge to participate successfully as a responsible 501(c)3 organization that contributes to the Kingdom work of God.

Made in the USA
Middletown, DE
15 March 2025

72627553R00079